D1217712

THE PERSIAN GULF AT THE DAWN OF THE NEW MILLENNIUM

THE PERSIAN GULF AT THE DAWN OF THE NEW MILLENNIUM

GAWDAT BAHGAT

Nova Science Publishers, Inc.
Huntington, New York

Editorial Production:	Susan Boriotti
Office Manager:	Annette Hellinger
Graphics:	Frank Grucci and Jennifer Lucas
Information Editor:	Tatiana Shohov
Book Production:	Patrick Davin, Cathy DeGregory, Donna Dennis, Jennifer Kuenzig, Christine Mathosian, Tammy Sauter and Lynette Van Helden
Circulation:	Lisa DeGangi and Michael Pazy Mino

Library of Congress Cataloging-in-Publication Data
Bahgat, Gawdat
The Persian Gulf at the dawn of the new millennium / Gawdat Bahgat.
      p.   cm.
Includes bibliographical references and index.
ISBN 1-56072-678-4
1. Persian Gulf Region—Politics and government. 2. Persian Gulf Region—Economic conditions. I. Title.
DS326.B254   1999   99-25142
953—dc21   CIP

Copyright 2000 by Nova Science Publishers, Inc.
  227 Main Street, Suite 100
  Huntington, New York 11743
  Tele. 631-424-6682Fax 631-424-4666
  e-mail: Novascience@earthlink.net
  e-mail: Novascil@aol.com
  Web Site: http://www.nexusworld.com/nova

Printed in the United States of America

CONTENTS

LIST OF TABLES

Chapter 1

OIL IN THE GULF:
PROSPECTS FOR THE NEW MILLENNIUM

In the closing years of the twentieth century the world continues to see growing demand for energy. Sources such as oil, natural gas, coal, nuclear, electricity, and some renewables have been utilized to satisfy this rising consumption. For the foreseeable future, there is little doubt that the global appetite for more energy will continue. Since the end of the Second World War oil has occupied a central stage in the international energy market. During these years, the oil industry has witnessed several significant changes concerning pricing, supply, demand, and reserves. The developments in all these areas have re-emphasized the crucial impact of the Persian Gulf producers on the dynamics of oil policy.

Since the mid-1970s the North Sea has emerged as a significant competitor to the Persian Gulf. More recently, the Caspian Basin has attracted tremendous attention as a major player in the global energy market. This chapter acknowledges the important contribution of these two regions. Nevertheless, the contention of the foregoing analysis is that, for the foreseeable future, the Gulf producers, particularly Saudi Arabia, are likely to regain their power in the oil industry. In the twenty-first century the world economy will depend more on oil supplies from the region. For reasons to be discussed shortly, the North Sea and Caspian Basin cannot replace the Gulf as the dominant player in energy politics.

The first part of this chapter provides a historical survey of the discovery of oil in the Persian Gulf and the tension between domestic forces and international companies over the ownership of these resources. Thereafter, the price fluctuations from 1973 to 1998 will be examined. In the following two sections the dynamics of both the demand and supply policies will be analyzed. In the concluding portion an attempt is made to demonstrate the unique characteristics of the Gulf that will keep it as the major player in the oil industry well into the twenty-first century.

THE EVOLUTION OF THE OIL INDUSTRY
IN THE PERSIAN GULF

The roots of the oil industry in the Persian Gulf go back to 1908 when oil was discovered at Mesjid-e Suleiman in southwest Iran[1]. In the following year the Anglo-Persian Oil Company was formed[2] and took charge of the extraction and marketing of the Iranian oil for the next several decades. The beginning of the First World War contributed, among other developments, to the rapid expansion of oil facilities in Iran. Shortly after the war oil was found in Iraq and in the 1930s it was discovered in Bahrain, Kuwait, Saudi Arabia, and later in the other Gulf states.[3] By World War II, the Gulf's share of world oil was not significant but the region's potential capabilities and reserves were apparent. The materialization of these capabilities had to wait until the end of the conflict. In the few decades following World War II, the Gulf producers have become prominent players in the global oil market. This market had been dominated by the so-called "Seven Sisters.[4]" The acceleration of oil exploration and production in the Gulf was necessary for the economic recovery of Western Europe and Japan throughout most of the 1950s and

---

[1] John Marlowe, *The Persian Gulf in the Twentieth Century*, New York: Frederick A. Praeger, 1962, p.80.)

[2] In 1935 the company was renamed the Anglo-Iranian oil company, in 1954 the name changed again to British Petroleum.

[3] Keith McLachian, "Oil in the Persian Gulf Area," in *The Persian Gulf States: A General Survey*, (ed.), Alvin J. Cottrell, Baltimore: Johns Hopkins University Press, 1980, pp. 200-204.

[4] These are Standard Oil of New Jersey (which changed its name to Exxon in 1972 and markets it products in Europe under the name Esso), the Royal Dutch/Shell group, Texaco, Standard Oil of California (known and marketed as Chevron), Mobil, Gulf Oil (which was purchased by Chevron), and British Petroleum. Another important company is Compagnie Francaise des Petroles (marketing as Total but known as Total-CFP since 1985).

1960s. During this period the industrialized world grew dependent on cheap and steady oil supplies from the Gulf. This dependence was fueled by the launching of the European Recovery Program, known as the Marshall Plan.[5] Thus, the Persian Gulf's share of world oil production jumped from 15.1 percent in 1951 to 31.9 percent in 1971.[6] Meanwhile, oil revenues have become the main source of income for all of the region's producing states.

This rising importance of oil in the indigenous economies coupled with foreign control by the international oil companies became issues in rising Arab and Iranian nationalism. The development in Iran in the early 1950s can be seen as an illustration of this conflict between domestic perceptions and foreign interests. After leading a campaign for the nationalization of the oil industry, Muhammad Mossadeq was elected as Iran's prime minister in 1951. His attempt to eliminate the Anglo-Iranian Oil Company's heavy dominance of the country's economy ended in failure in 1953 when he was overthrown by a coup d'etat supported by foreign powers. For most of the following two decades there was no repeat of the Mossadeq experiment in any of the Persian Gulf states. Instead, a less confrontational attitude was adopted by the Gulf governments in their long negotiations with the oil companies. Several agreements were reached between the two sides that gradually increased the power of the oil-producer states. These include the 50-50 arrangement by which companies agreed to pay the local governments 50 percent of profits[7] and the Tehran Agreement of 1971 under which companies agreed to a price revision.[8] Finally, in the 1970s most of the companies' assets were taken over by the local governments. In the process, the Organization of the Petroleum Exporting Countries (OPEC) was created in 1960 by five original members: Iran, Iraq, Kuwait, Saudi Arabia, and Venezuela.[9] An important objective for

---

[5] Geoffrey Kemp and Robert E. Harkavy, *Strategic Geography and the Changing Middle East*, Washington DC: Brookings Institution, 1997, p.49.

[6] British Petroleum (BP), *BP Statistical Review of World Energy*, London: British Petroleum Company, various years.

[7] Fred Halliday, *Arabia without Sultans*, New York: Vintage Books, 1975, p.417.

[8] *Europa Publications, The Middle East and North Africa*, London: Staples Printers Rochester Limited, 1996, p.123.

[9] Between 1960 and 1975, OPEC expanded to 13 members with the addition of Qatar, Indonesia, Libya, United Arab Emirates, Algeria, Nigeria, Ecuador, and Gabon. Currently, the organization consists of 11 member nations (Ecuador dropped out in December 1992 and Gabon withdrew effective January 1995).

OPEC has been to coordinate members' petroleum policies and to protect their interests in their confrontation with the companies.[10] The showdown between the two sides came in the aftermath of the Arab-Israeli war of 1973.

PRICE SHOCKS

For most of the two decades following the end of World War II, oil prices were stable at very low level. This cheap price had two intertwined impacts on energy consumption. On one hand, the share of oil in world energy increased at the expense of its then main competitor-coal. On the other hand, the industrial world became more dependent on oil. Indeed, many analysts credit the economic recovery in Western Europe and Japan to low oil prices.[11] The developments in the 1970s drastically altered the dynamics of the global oil market. Since 1973 oil prices have been highly volatile as the following table shows.

Table I
Oil Prices (1972-1997) US dollars per barrel

Year	$	Year	$	Year	$
1972	01.90	1981	34.32	1990	20.50
1973	02.83	1982	31.80	1991	16.56
1974	10.41	1983	28.78	1992	17.21
1975	10.70	1984	28.07	1993	14.90
1976	11.63	1985	27.53	1994	14.76
1977	12.38	1986	12.97	1995	16.09
1978	13.03	1987	16.92	1996	18.56
1979	29.75	1988	13.22	1997	18.14
1980	35.69	1989	15.69		

Source: The British Petroleum, *BP Statistical Review of World Energy* 1998, London: The British Petroleum Company, 1998, p.14.

---

[10] For a recent assessment of OPEC, see Jahangir Amuzegar, "OPEC's Seventh Life," *Middle East Policy*, Vol.5, No.3, September 1997, pp.25-40. Also the Organization's website www.opec.org.

[11] For example, see Geoffrey Kemp, *Energy Superbowl: Strategic Politics and the Persian Gulf and Caspian Basin*, Washington D.C.: Nixon Center for Peace and Freedom, 1997.

This price volatility is explained by interruptions of supplies from the Persian Gulf due to political crises. The sharp rise of oil prices in the aftermath of 1973 October War between the Arabs and Israel represented a traumatic break with the past. In addition to the jump in prices, the producer states demonstrated their newly gained power at the expense of the international oil companies. In response, the consumer governments in the Organization for Economic Cooperation and Development (OECD) created the International Energy Agency (IEA).[12] The participating countries decided to take several measures to avoid another oil shock. These include holding stocks equivalent to 90 days of net oil imports, demand restraint, and fuel switching.[13] These measures, however, did not prevent the second oil shock which came in late 1970s as a reaction to the political turmoil in Iran. The instability that accompanied the overthrow of the Shah and the establishment of the Islamic regime resulted in a sharp decline in oil output. In 1978 Iran produced 5.3 million barrels per day (b/d); three years later (1981), the level dropped to 1.4 million b/d.[14] In response to the shortage of oil supplies, prices skyrocketed to an unprecedented level of $35.69 per barrel.[15] This volatility of prices reinforced the trend toward energy conservation in many western and importing countries. In other words, the apparent vulnerability of industrialized nations to the interruption of oil supplies from the Persian Gulf incited efforts to cut back the growth in per capita energy consumption.[16] According to the IEA, in 1993 the European members in the OECD used approximately 20 percent less energy per unit of gross domestic product

---

[12] France participated in the discussions in 1974 leading to the formation of the IEA but decided not to join. It subsequently cooperated with the IEA policies and became a member in 1992.

[13] William F. Martin, Ryikichi Imai, and Helga Steeg, *Maintaining Energy Security in a Global Context*, New York: The Trilateral Commission, 1996, p.14.

[14] US Department of Energy, Energy Information Administration (EIA), *International Petroleum Statistics Report*, Washington D.C.: Government Printing Office, August 1997, p.38.

[15] British Petroleum, *BP Statistical Review of World Energy*, London, British Petroleum Company, 1998, p.14.

[16] Joshua S. Goldstein, Xiaoming Huang, and Burcu Akan, "Energy in the World Economy, 1950-92," *International Studies Quarterly*, Vol.41, No.2, 1997, p.245.

(GDP) than in 1971.[17] Similarly, in the United States oil intensity fell but less than in Europe, which has higher taxes on petroleum products.

The Iraqi invasion of Kuwait in 1990 resulted in the withdrawal of the two countries' production from the world oil market. However, this time the world was better prepared to deal with this shortage of supplies. There was a cushion of unused capacity and in a short time Saudi Arabia was able to increase its production to make up for the Iraqi (and temporarily the Kuwaiti) oil. Thus, the Saudi production jumped from 5.06 million in 1989 to 8.33 million barrels per day in 1992.[18] It is to be remembered that the kingdom had asserted its leading role in determining prices in the mid 1980s. The 1986 price plunge occurred when Saudi Arabia shifted from a policy of holding its production down in the interest of price stability (what is known as "swing producer,") to one of exporting more of its low-cost oil in order to gain market share. Consequently, a major oil price shock was avoided.

Furthermore, for most of the 1970s and 1980s prices reflected an intense competition between two strategies within the producer countries. One group of countries led by Saudi Arabia favored maintaining stable or relatively low prices, and keeping output at the level required to sustain these prices. These states were characterized by small populations, large reserves, and large capital surpluses. The main goal for this policy was to reduce incentives for consumer countries to switch to other sources of energy or to seek oil from other producers. A contrasting stand was adopted by countries (such as Iran and Iraq) with large populations and extensive development programs. In general they favored high prices to implement their ambitious development plans.[19]

Since the early 1990s prices have been relatively steady at levels below (in real terms) those of the mid 1970s. This relative stability of oil prices was shattered in late 1997 and the early 1998 when prices plunged to the lowest level in a decade. In addition to the warm winter in the North, the so-called

---

[17] International Energy Agency, (IEA), *World Energy Outlook*, Paris: IEA, 1996, p.91.

[18] US Department of Energy, Energy Information Administration, *International Petroleum Statistics* Report, Washington D.C.: Government Printing Office, May 1997, p.38.

[19] Abbas Alnasrawi, "Oil Dimensions of the Gulf Crisis," in Ibrahim Ibrahim, (ed.), *The Gulf Crisis: Background and Consequences*, Washington D.C.: Georgetown University Press, 1992, p.43.

"El Nino" effect, this huge drop can be explained by two developments, one on the supply side and the other on the demand side. First, OPEC's share of world oil supply had remained constant between 1993 and 1996 as non-OPEC supply had increased dramatically. Thus, in an effort to regain some of is influence, OPEC ministers met in Jakarta, Indonesia in November 1997 and approved their first increase in the overall production quota since 1993. The organization's production rose by 10 percent from 25 million b/d to 27.5 million b/d. This increased OPEC's share of the world's oil supply by 1 percentage point.[20] Saudi officials believed that global demand would rise by 2 million b/d in 1998 and that non-OPEC output would only increase by 1 million b/d.[21] In other words, the decision to raise production can be seen as an attempt by Saudi Arabia to meet growing global demand. Second, almost at the same time OPEC decided to raise production the world oil market was stunned by the Asia's financial problems. For the last several years the Southeast Asian economies' demand for oil was growing by nearly 6 percent annually (in comparison with a worldwide rate of 1.7 percent.[22] Asian economic problems are likely to continue to slow down the region's rapid growth rate and reduce its demand of oil.[23]

In response to this combination of expanding production and shrinking demand, oil prices fell from $22 a barrel in October 1997 to $12.80 a barrel by mid-March 1998.[24] In order to contain this unexpected deterioration of oil prices several meetings were held between OPEC members and between them and other non-OPEC producing countries such as Mexico. These efforts resulted in the so-called Riyadh Pact (a cut in output of 1.245 million b/d) and Amsterdam Pact (a cut of 450,000 b/d).[25] In late June 1998 OPEC members met in Vienna and announced plans to reduce their production by more than

---

[20] US Department of Energy, Energy Information Administration (EIA), *OPEC Fact Sheet*, Washington D.C.: Government Printing Office, May 1998, p.3.

[21] *Energy Economist*, "Energy Market Report," No. 194, December 1997, p.25.

[22] Tom Manning, "Asian Financial Crisis to Slow Growth in Global Oil Demand," *Oil & Gas Journal*, Vol.96, No.18, May 4, 1998, p.41.

[23] In the last several years Asian economies had added approximately 800,000 b/d to each year's growth in worldwide oil demand. See *Oil and Gas Journal*, "The Oil Market's Whiplash," Vol.96, No.13, March 30, 1998, p.21.

[24] *Middle East Monitor*, "Saudi Arabia Leads Efforts on OPEC and non-OPEC Production Cut," Vol.28, No.3, March 1998, p.15.

[25] *Reuters on line*, "Oil Ministers to Begin Quest for Further Cuts," June 5, 1998.

1.3 million b/d in addition to the two previous cuts.[26] By taking these steps OPEC producers hope to put prices back on the "right" track. Whether this will happen or not depends on how strict the participants will adhere to their commitments as well as on other factors that will be analyzed in the next sections.

To sum up, three conclusions can be drawn from the foregoing analysis of oil prices since the early 1970s. First, there is a strong correlation between the level of oil output in the Persian Gulf and the volatility of prices. The fluctuations of production over the last three decades should be seen more as a response to changes in the political and security environment in the region and less as a reaction to economic forces. This fact suggests that stability in the Gulf region is an essential requirement to guarantee the flow of oil supplies and to avoid another jump in prices. Second, it is important to point out that oil shocks produced more than shortage of supplies. The rise in prices in 1973 and 1979 caused widespread disturbances of global economies including high levels of inflation and unemployment. The recovery proved slow and painful. This conclusion leads to the third conclusion or issue-oil security. The prosperity of the consumer states does not mean achieving a greater self-sufficiency in oil or reaching a state of "energy independence.[27]" The high level of interdependence among world economies means that it does not really make a great difference who buys and who sells a barrel of oil, but an interruption of supplies hurts all economies.

For the foreseeable future fluctuations of oil prices are not likely to be sustained for a long period of time. A prolonged sharp rise would intensify efforts for energy conservation and reduce the growth of demand. A severe drop of prices for a prolonged period could destabilize the economic and political systems in the Gulf-an undesirable outcome. Thus, in the beginning of the twenty-first century a slow and incremental rise of oil prices can be expected. Indeed, the US Department of Energy projects that oil prices will

---

[26] Youssef M. Ibrahim, "OPEC Reaches New Deal to Cut Oil Production," New York Times, June 25, 1998, p.D1.

[27] Edward R. Fried and Philip H. Trezise, *Oil Security: Retrospect and Prospect*, Washington D.C.: The Brookings Institution, 1993, p.5.

reach about $22.00 (constant 1996 US dollars) per barrel by the year 2020.[28] This forecast is based on the expected changes in both demand and supply.

THE GROWING DEMAND

After a short period of flat demand growth in the late 1980s and the early 1990s, oil consumption has been on the rise. In the closing years of the twentieth century virtually all observers of the industry agree that oil demand will grow for the foreseeable future.[29] This can be explained by the significant advantages oil retains over other forms of energy particularly in regard to the pre-supply infrastructure investment and the easiness of shipping it from the fields to the markets. In addition, oil still is the most convenient fuel for transportation. Not surprisingly, world oil consumption is projected to increase over the next several years and will vary from one region to another as the following table demonstrates

Table II
World Oil Consumption by Region 2000-2020 Million Barrels per Day

Region/Country	1995	2000	2020	Average Annual Percent Change1995-2020
United States	17.7	19.6	024.4	1.3
Western Europe	14.1	14.3	015.4	0.3
Japan	05.7	06.3	008.0	1.4
Total Industrialized	42.4	45.6	055.3	1.1
Asia	11.3	13.3	028.6	3.8
China	03.3	04.4	011.2	5.0
India	01.6	01.8	003.8	3.6
Africa	02.3	03.1	005.1	3.2
Total Developing	21.6	26.0	050.6	3.5
World	69.9	77.5	116.1	2.0

Source: US Department of Energy, Energy Information Administration, *International Energy Outlook*, Washington D.C.: Government Printing Office, 1998, p.136.

---

[28] US Department of Energy, Energy Information Administration (EIA), *International Energy Outlook*, Washington DC: Government Printing Office, 1998, p.2.

[29] Paul Stevens, "Oil Prices: The Start of an Era?" *Energy Policy*, Vol.24, No.5, May 1996, p.394.

The major explanation of increasing demand is improved economic conditions. The demand for oil is highly income elastic. In other words, when individuals and nations get richer, their energy consumption rises. From 1985 to 1995 per capita average annual growth rate in the gross national product (GNP) of South-east Asian countries was 7.2 percent while that of the industrialized world was 1.9 percent.[30] This variation in the level of economic growth partly explains the differences between the two regions in their demand for energy. Thus, the large gap in oil consumption between the industrialized "North" and the developing "South" is expected to shrink in the coming century. Still, different forces will shape the future of energy consumption in each region.

Energy conservation (energy consumption per unit of GDP) has been an important concern for many industrialized countries since the early 1970s. This interest in energy efficiency has been fueled by two developments: the interruptions of oil supplies from the Persian Gulf and the growing concern about the environment. The combination of these two factors resulted in an improvement in energy intensity in most of the industrialized nations over the last 20 years. This trend toward conservation was reinforced by the signing of the Kyoto Protocol in December 1997 when countries from all over the world agreed to a new set of commitments for reducing greenhouse gas emissions. If the industrialized nations adhere to this agreement, their demand for oil should be considerably restrained.

On the other hand, the consumption of oil in the developing world, particularly in South-east Asian states, is projected to grow.[31] The region's demand for oil rose by 7.7 million b/d between 1986 and 1996 accounting for 83 percent of global increase. Thus, South-east Asian economies have already become an important force in the global oil market and the world economy in general. Not surprisingly, international financial institutions rushed to assist the region to overcome the economic crisis of late 1997 and early 1998, particularly the countries that have been harmed the most-South Korea, Indonesia, Thailand, and Malaysia. Many analysts believe that in a short time

---

[30] The World Bank, *World Development Report*, New York: Oxford University Press, 1997, p.215.

[31] For a detailed discussion see Mamdouh G. Salameh, "The geopolitics of oil in the Asia-Pacific region and its strategic implications," *OPEC Review*, Vol.21, No.2, June 1997, pp.125-131.

those countries will recover and resume their economic growth, albeit at a slower rate. A recent study by the London-based Center for Global Energy Studies predicts that Asian oil consumption will grow at a rate of 3.1 to 5.1 percent a year from now to 2010.[32] Most of the demand will be met by production from the Gulf. In this regard, China's soaring economic growth and, consequently, demand for energy deserves special attention.

Two characteristics can explain Beijing's growing demand of oil: its huge population and its sustained economic growth. Thus, in spite of sizeable oil production the country has been a net importer since the mid 1990s.[33] Unlike other Asian states, the recent economic downturn has little impact on the Chinese economy. This suggests that there will be few restraints on China's oil demand in the foreseeable future. In order to satisfy this growing consumption Beijing will have to rely on supplies from the Gulf, the Caspian Basin, and other sources. This raises the question of the availability and reliability of supplies.

THE AVAILABILITY AND RELIABILITY OF OIL SUPPLIES

In 1974 the share of the Persian Gulf in world oil production reached a peak of 36.2 percent.[34] Since then the structure of the international market has changed. Suppliers from outside the Gulf have increased their output at the expense of Gulf producers. The prices shocks and the fear of political disruptions of oil supplies from the region incited efforts to explore and develop other sources. In addition, two developments have contributed to the expansion of the oil market. First, the continuous and sweeping improvement in technology has increased the number of producers. Subsea drilling innovation has permitted access to resource-rich, deepwater areas that were considered economically not worthy or environmentally too risky for development. Consequently, significant offshore additions to the resource

---

[32] David Knott, "Asian Oil Demand Set for Recovery," *Oil and Gas Journal*, Vol.96, No.17, April 27, 1998, p.23.

[33] For an analysis of the Asian and Chinese oil policy see Kent E. Calder, "Asia's Empty Tank," *Foreign Affairs*, Vol.75, No.2, March/April 1996, pp.55-69.

[34] US Department of Energy, EIA, *International Petroleum Statistics Report*, Washington D.C.: Government Printing Office, May 1996, p.43.

base have been achieved in North America, the North Sea, and Africa. Indeed, offshore oil has provided almost all of the world's increased hydrocarbon supplies during the past 20 years.[35] Second, the end of the Cold War removed the political barriers for the international oil companies to explore and develop old and new sources. Thus, renewed efforts and vast amounts of money have been invested in areas such as Vietnam, China, and, most important, the Caspian Basin.

The outcome of these two developments has been a sustained substantial increase in world oil output since the late 1970s. This prompted a prominent analyst to conclude that "rather than a world which is running out of oil, as was so widely forecast in the early 1970s, the world has been running into it.[36]" The bulk of this "new oil" has been coming from the North Sea. According to the International Energy Agency, North Sea oil supply expansion accounted for almost all the supply increase in the Organization for Economic Cooperation and Development (OECD) and over three quarters of the non-OPEC supply increase outside of the former Soviet Union in the period 1992 to 1995.[37]

This impressive development of oil resources from the North Sea is considered by many analysts as the most significant achievement in the global market over the last two decades. The utilization of this hydrocarbon wealth is attributed mainly to technological advancements. These include three-dimensional

(3-D) seismic, four-dimensional (4-D) or time-dependent seismic, improved water injection techniques, and horizontal drilling.[38] These advance innovations have had a twofold impact on the development of oil fields in the North Sea. First, they reduced the cost of production and, second, they

---

[35] Matthew R. Simmons, "Failure to recognize depletion may harm long-term supply," *Petroleum Economist*, Vol.64, No.9, September 1997, p.50.

[36] Peter R. Odell, "Oil Reserves: Much More than Meets the Eye," *Petroleum Economist*, Vol.64, No.11, November 1997, p.29.

[37] International Energy Agency, *World Energy Outlook*, Paris: International Energy Agency, 1996, p.29.

[38] Seismic 3-D uses fast computing and improved graphic techniques. It has improved identification of oil in place in old fields that conventional techniques have passed over. Seismic 4-D identifies drainage patterns over time and locates by-passed oil. See Anthony J. Finizza, "The Future of Oil," *Business Economics*, October 1996, p.10.

contributed to the discovery of new fields and the longevity of old ones. In short, it can be stated that technology has been a major reason for the soaring output from the North Sea for the last 20 years. In addition, the region provides an attractive investment environment, an advanced fiscal regime, and a secure legal system. Comparing the North Sea with the Gulf, the former enjoys a more stable legal, financial, and political climate than the latter.

Technology, investment environment, and oil price levels explain how the North Sea has attracted and secured the bulk of international investment since the late 1970s.[39] Ironically, the region holds only about 2 percent of world proven reserves.[40] Thus, paradoxically, this high level of productivity in conjunction with poor reserves will lead to the depletion of oil fields in the North Sea in the not very long term. It is estimated that the production of Norway and the United Kingdom (where most of the oil is concentrated) will peak early in the next century then gradually decline. These limited reserves raise doubt about future supplies from the region in the future.

Unlike the North Sea, the Caspian Basin is believed to enjoy tremendous reserves. The estimates for the region's reserves vary widely but most analysts agree that Caspian resources seem very promising. Thus, for the last several years it has been considered as a major next axis in the worldwide energy supply. However, the problem in utilizing these attractive resources is not geological. Rather, numerous political obstacles must be overcome in a timely fashion in order to develop them, particularly the questions of ownership and transportation.

First, in the question of ownership, the five littoral states (Russia, Iran, Azerbaijan, Turkmenistan, and Kazakhstan) do not agree on the legal status of the basin. If it is classed as a sea, then it should be divided up into national sectors like the North Sea and developed independently. But if it is designated as a lake, it should be treated as a joint property shared by all bordering states. Given the fact that few discoveries have been made on the Russian and the Iranian shores, these two countries advocate the perception of the Caspian as a lake while the other three states view it as a sea. Early in 1998 Russia made a

---

[39] It is estimated that three quarters of total worldwide oil investment are spent in the North Sea. See Paul Tempest, "Oil Supply Prospects: A Confused and Shifting Pattern," *Middle East International*, No.526, May 10, 1996, p.20.

[40] British Petroleum, *BP Statistical Review of World Energy*, London: British Petroleum Company, 1998, p.4.

crucial shift in its position. It agreed that the seabed and the mineral reserves beneath it could be divided entirely into national sectors although it wanted the seawaters to be managed jointly by all five nations.[41] By mid-1998, there has not been change in the Iranian position. To sum up, the question of who owns what in the Caspian Sea needs to be resolved by negotiations among the five littoral states in order to remove this legal obstacle.

Second is pipeline diplomacy, Most of the states in the region are land-locked. For their oil to reach the international market it has to pass through the territory of at least one other country. Most of the current pipelines go through Russia. Most of the other proposed routes are blocked in virtually every direction by dissident and separatist activity of civil wars (Chechnya, Abkhazia, and Nagorno-Karabakh) and by the US policy of containing Iran, thus denying it a role as a transit country. In the closing years of the 1990s, several pipeline schemes have been under discussion. The construction of several of them is already under way.

In summary, the Caspian Basin holds tremendous hydrocarbon resources but, given the political problems within and outside the region, it is far from clear when and if these resources will be fully utilized.[42] This high level of uncertainty regarding the future of the North Sea and the Caspian Basin highlights the significance of the Persian Gulf as the major world oil reservoir both at present and in the foreseeable future.

THE GULF: PROSPECTS AND PROBLEMS

Despite the increasing worldwide oil output over the last two decades, the Persian Gulf is still considered the crucial player in the industry. Equally important, for the future the region is projected to be more significant. This can be explained by three characteristics. First, unlike the North Sea producing states, the Gulf countries hold huge reserves as the following table shows.

---

[41] *The Economist*, "Caspian Carve-up," Vol.346, No.8058, March 7, 1998, p.66.

[42] For a thorough analysis see Rosemarie Forsythe, *The Politics of Oil in the Caucasus and Central Asia*, Adelphi Paper No.300, New York: Oxford University Press, 1996.

Table III
Proven Oil Reserves in Selected Countries, Year-End 1997

Country	Share of Total Reserve in billion barrels	Reserve to Proven Reserves %	Production Ratio*
Norway	10.4	1.0	8.6
UK	5.0	0.5	5.2
Iran	93.0	9.0	69.0
Iraq	112.5	10.8	100+
Kuwait	96.5	9.3	100+
Oman	5.2	0.5	15.8
Qatar	3.7	0.4	15.1
Saudi Arabia	261.5	25.2	79.5
UAE	97.8	9.4	100+

*Ratio of proven reserves to production is in years. Proven means that there is considerable geologic and engineering evidence that supports the ability to develop such resources under current economic and technological environments.
Source: British Petroleum, *BP Statistical Review of World Energy*, London: British Petroleum Company, 1998, p.4.

The figures show the wide disparity between reserves in the North Sea and the Gulf states. Second, unlike the Caspian Basin, oil fields in the Persian Gulf are located on well-developed transport routes. As has been discussed earlier, production on a commercial basis started in the Arab Gulf states after World War II and much earlier in Iran. Since then, an advanced infrastructure connecting the region with the global market has been established. It will take some time and large investment to create similar infrastructure in the Caspian Basin. Third, the costs to produce a barrel of oil in the Gulf are much lower than those in any other region in the world.[43] This means that there is a wider range of profit in the Gulf than the rest of the world.

Putting all these advantages together, it is clear that in spite of advanced technology and better fiscal environment in other areas, the Gulf will remain

---

[43] It is estimated that the cost to produce a barrel of oil in the Persian Gulf ranges between $0.99 and $1.49 which is much lower than the cost of production in the rest of the world.

the major producing region in the world in the twenty-first century. However, in order to maintain this status fundamental obstacles need to be overcome. These include securing financial resources to expand production and the "rehabilitation" or "reintegration" of both Iraq and Iran into the international system.

Given the immense reserves the Gulf states hold, there is no doubt that the region has the capability to meet the growing world demand of oil. Simply stated, there is plenty of oil around. Nevertheless, it is not certain that required funding to expand production will be forthcoming. According to a senior Kuwaiti official, Arab Gulf states will need to invest about $200 billion in their energy sectors over the next decade to meet an expected worldwide increase in demand for oil.[44] For a long time, the oil industry in the region has been dominated by the local governments. Recent security crises such as the Iran-Iraq war (1980-1988), the Gulf War (1991), and the soaring military expenditures have wiped out a big proportion of the financial assets the region had accumulated in the early 1970s. Recently, attempts have been made by a number of Gulf states to provide incentives in order to attract private and foreign investment. A recent study by the International Monetary Fund (IMF) recommended that a broader privatization program aimed at creating a more efficient economic system should be geared toward higher private-sector activity and a further liberalization of foreign direct investment.[45] Not surprisingly, the Arab Gulf states with the lowest cash flows (Bahrain, Oman, and Qatar) are ahead of the others in terms of increasing incentives to attract sources of outside capital in their energy industries.[46] It still is too early to provide any assessment of the potential participation by private and foreign investments in the oil industry, but it is likely that more efforts will be made to achieve this goal.

Since Iran's Islamic Revolution in 1979 the relations between that country and the United States have deteriorated. In the last few years Washington has

---

[44] See a statement by Ali Hamad Al Bahar, the general manager of Kuwait Insurance Company, "Gulf Arabs Need $200 Billion to Boost Energy Sector," Reuters, May 11, 1998.

[45] Cyrus Sassanpour, *Policy Challenges in the Gulf Cooperation Council Countries*, Washington D.C.: International Monetary Fund, 1996, p.25.

[46] John Duke Anthony, "Special Report: Consultation and Consensus in Kuwait: The 18th GCC Summit," Middle East Policy, Vol.6, No.1, June 1998, p.149.

taken several measures to limit international investment in the Iranian energy sector. The Iran-Libya Sanctions Act (ILSA) of 1996 is a good illustration of this policy. These sanctions have partly succeeded in reducing the incentives for foreign investment in the Islamic Republic of Iran. However, several international oil companies have shown interest in the Iranian hydrocarbon sector in spite of the ILSA. The primary challenge came in 1997 when the French company Total along with Gazprom of Russia and Petronas of Malaysia signed an agreement with the National Iranian Oil Company (NIOC) to invest $2 billion to develop the giant South Pars field.[47] Iran needs to attract more funding to revive its oil industry. Senior economists predict that the country requires up to $90 billion in the next 10 years in order to maintain current levels of production.[48] Recently Iran has offered several buy-back projects to international firms.[49]

In early 1990 Iraq had plans to increase its output to 6 million b/d within a five-year period.[50] However, since the Iraqi invasion of Kuwait Baghdad has been allowed to export very little oil. Moreover, any attempt to modernize the hydrocarbon infrastructure has been frozen. In the early 1998 the Security Council of the United Nations authorized Iraq to sell more of its oil and to use of the revenues to update and modernize its hydrocarbon infrastructure. Still, there is no way to provide any credible prediction on when or how the Iraqi crisis might end. Rather, it is possible to assert that the country is a major player in the international oil market. When sanctions are lifted and Iraq is allowed to resume its role as a leading exporter country, it will need billions of dollars to repair its war-damaged infrastructure and pipelines. Many international companies have already shown interest in developing Iraq's oil capabilities once a political settlement is reached.[51] Another explanation for

---

[47] After long and hard negotiations with Europe, President Clinton agreed to waive the sanctions against these corporations.

[48] Afshin Molavi, "Iran Economy Faces New Year with Tough Challenges," Reuters on line, March 23, 1998.

[49] Under the buy-back formula, the outside company is required to put up all of the investment capital needed to fund the development project. Repayment of capital expenditures as well as some agreed-upon rate of remuneration is then recouped from the sale of oil from the venture.

[50] Energy Economist, "A Shift Worth Watching," No.192, October 1997, p.6.

[51] As of June 1997, there reportedly were almost 60 foreign oil companies from a wide variety of countries that were in discussions with the Iraqi government including

Iran's nuclear ambitions is Israel. Since the Shah was overthrown in 1979 Jerusalem and Tehran have been strong enemies to each other. Israel is believed by most observers and intelligence agencies to be a nuclear power. As had been illustrated in the Israeli attack against the Iraqi reactor in 1981, Jerusalem would not hesitate to use all means, including the military ones, to prevent the emergence of another nuclear power in the Middle East. The Iranians seriously believe that Israel would attack their nuclear facilities. Developments in the late 1990s raise the stakes in this growing hostility between the Jewish state and the Islamic Republic. According to some reports Israel has been cultivating secret intelligence contacts with the

In conclusion, in the twenty-first century the world will grow more dependent on oil supplies from the Persian Gulf. The region enjoys more advantages in terms of reserves, costs, and location than any other area in the world. For the Gulf states to produce at their full capacity, private and foreign funding will be required. In addition, both Iran and Iraq will have to be fully reintegrated into the global system. There is no guarantee that any of these steps will be taken, but the stakes are very high and substantial efforts need to be made to achieve this goal.

Russian, Chinese, French and even US firms. See US Department of Energy, Energy Information Administration (EIA), Country Analysis Briefs-Iraq, Washington D.C.: Government Printing Office, February 1998, p.9.

Chapter 2

STABILITY IN THE PERSIAN GULF: THE WATER DIMENSION

For several decades oil has been the main source of energy used by man. This worldwide dependence on oil is expected to endure for many years to come. Since the 1950s, the Gulf region has emerged as a major producer and its significance in satisfying the world's growing appetite for oil is increasing due to the region's immense proven reserves. Thus, the stability of the eight Gulf states - Bahrain, Iran, Iraq, Kuwait, Oman, Qatar, Saudi Arabia, and the United Arab Emirates (UAE) - has become an important concern for the global powers in order to secure oil supplies from the region. The Gulf war and its aftermath can be seen as an illustration of the international community's determination to contain any threat to the region. This heavy Western military presence in the Gulf since the early 1990s has ensured the non-interrupted flow of oil shipments from the region. However, putting the external threats aside, the Gulf states face tremendous internal challenges.

In addition to the ideological differences (conservative monarchies, Islamism, and radical nationalism), ethnic division (Arabs and Kurds), and sectarian split (Sunnis and Shi'is) the environmental make-up of the region contributes to a growing tendency towards polarization and conflict. The climate in most of the Gulf states is either arid or semi-arid. As a result, the region receives very little rain annually. The average annual rainfall in the six Gulf monarchies is only 84.5 mm.[52].

According to the United Nations, an annual amount of one thousand cubic meters per capita represents the so-called "water-barrier," the minimum level

---

[52] Peter H. Gleick, (ed.), Water in Crisis: A Guide to the World's Fresh Water Resources, New York: Oxford University Press, 1993, p.141.

to sustain a reasonable way of life.[53] Any amount below this level is considered inadequate and can expose the inhabitants to social, economic, and health challenges. Most of the people in the Gulf receive far less water than recommended by the UN. In addition, the prospects for an improvement in the foreseeable future are dim.

The underlying reason for the water shortage in the Gulf is the fact that the consumption is growing at a faster rate than the replenishing process. Over the last few decades, this situation has been aggravated by a combination of two developments. Both of them are, more or less, related to the increase in oil prices. In less than a generation, the population of the Gulf has more than doubled as the following table shows.

Table I
Population Growth in the Persian Gulf States

Country	Annual growth rate			
	1960	1994	2000	1960-1994
Bahrain	00.2	00.5	00.6	3.7
Iran	21.6	66.7	76.4	3.4
Iraq	06.8	19.6	23.1	3.2
Kuwait	00.3	01.8	02.0	5.6
Oman	00.6	02.1	02.7	4.0
Qatar	00.1	00.5	00.6	7.6
S. Arabia	04.1	17.8	21.7	4.4
UAE	00.1	02.2	02.4	9.8
World				1.8

*Columns 2, 3, and 4 are in millions of people.
Source: United Nations Development Program, *Human Development Report*, New York: Oxford University Press, 1997, table 22, pp.194-195.

More users means less water for everyone. Moreover, these rapidly growing inhabitants enjoy higher standard of living than their predecessors which also leads to more consumption. Thus, over the last several years the shortage of water in the Gulf region has become more acute and,

---

[53] United Nations Environment Program, *World Resources*, New York: Oxford University Press, 1996, p.302.

consequently, the awareness of the problem has increased. Still, governments' efforts to narrow the growing gap between water-demand and water-availability have achieved very modest success, if any. By the closing years of this century, all the indicators point to a deeper and multi-dimensional water problem in the Gulf.

In addition to scarcity the water-map in the region has two other characteristics which complicate the situation even further. First, there is a serious maldistribution of water resources all over the region. The six monarchies have very little water, both surface and underground. Iran and Iraq, on the other side, are, relatively speaking, much better off than their neighbors. Second, most of these water-resources are trans-borders, expanding in a large area regardless of the political boundaries between the modern-day nation states. These characteristics of water resources in the Gulf (importance, scarcity, maldistribution, and being shared) have made any attempt to find a "national" solution obsolete. A more comprehensive regional approach is a necessity particularly in order to alleviate the impact of long-term and widespread mismanagement and lack of planning.

Water problems facing the Gulf states are not identical. Rather, two salient ones can be identified and will be examined. These are the Iraqi dependence on water resources located outside its boundaries and the severe shortage of water supplies in the six Gulf monarchies. The magnitude of each problem will be analyzed as well as the different approaches to deal with them. finally, an attempt is made to shed light on the future of "water-policy" in the foreseeable future.

IRAQ'S WATER VULNERABILITY

Unlike the six Gulf monarchies, Iraq does not suffer from a severe water-shortage. Rather, Baghdad has a variety of sources to satisfy its needs including an average annual rainfall of about 800 mm ranging from less than 150 mm in the south-western desert to over 1,892 mm in the mountains of the north-east[54]; two important rivers: Euphrates and Tigris; and aquifers. Still, Iraq faces a water-problem of a different magnitude and different kind. Its

---

[54] Natasha Beschorner, *Water and Instability in the Middle East*, London: Brassey's, 1993, p.34.

most important sources, the Euphrates and the Tigris rivers, originate mainly from outside its borders. Approximately %98 of the Euphrates originates in the mountains of eastern Anatolia and about %50 of the Tigris rises from there as well. Other attributes to the Tigris are located in Iraq with their headquarters in Iran including the Greater and Lesser Zab, the Adheim, and the Diyala rivers.[55] Meanwhile, %40 of the Euphrates lies in Turkey, %25 in Syria, and %35 in Iraq, and %20 of the Tigris lies in Turkey, %78 in Iraq, and only %2 in the northeastern corner of Syria.[56] This leaves Baghdad dependent on and vulnerable to its neighbors: Turkey and Syria on the Euphrates, and Turkey and Iran on the Tigris. Over the years, this dependence has deepened Iraq's sense of national vulnerability and contributed to its feeling of insecurity.

A close examination of the Iraqi water resources justifies this fear. First, as the most down-stream riparian on the Euphrates, Baghdad has been at the mercy of both Syria and Turkey. As will be discussed shortly, Baghdad's demands of what it perceives as its fair share of the Euphrates have often collided with those of Damascus and Ankara. The latter has tremendous leverage over the basin and has not shown any hesitation in taking full advantage of its strong position as the upstream riparian. Second, in contrast to the Euphrates, a smaller part of the Tigris rises from outside Iraq. However, the fact that Iraq is less vulnerable to external control over the Tigris should not be taken as comfort to the government in Baghdad. A serious challenge should be taken into consideration. Most of the Tigris's attributes in Iraq are located in the northeastern part of the country where the majority of the population is Kurds.[57] Given the unstable conditions there in the last few decades, it is apparent that water from the Tigris can not be taken for granted either. Third, since water supplies from the twin rivers are threatened, one by both Syria and Turkey, and the other by the Kurds, other sources have to be considered. However, it is important to point out that Iraq's ground-water

---

[55] Natasha Beschorner, *Water and Instability in the Middle East*, London: Brassey's, 1992, p.29.

[56] Daniel Hillel, Rivers of Eden: *The Struggle for Water and the Quest for Peace in the Middle East*, New York: Oxford University Press, 1994, p.92.

[57] Thomas Naff, "Sources of Potential Conflict in the Persian Gulf: The Water Factor," in Geoffrey Kempt and Janice Gross Stein, (eds.), *Powder Keg in the Middle East*, Lanham, MD: Rowman and Littlefield, 1995, p.311.

resources are limited and underdeveloped. These supplies can not make up for any loss of water from the two rivers. Moreover, unlike the other seven Gulf states, Iraq is almost a landlocked state with a very narrow outlet on the Gulf which means that the availability of water from there for desalination is very limited. In short, it can be stated that Baghdad depends heavily on the two rivers, Euphrates and Tigris, to satisfy its water needs. The other sources are inadequate. However, the reliability of uninterrupted flow from the two rivers, particularly the Euphrates, can not be taken for granted and for the last several years Turkey has already taken several steps which caused a slow of the flow of the Euphrates to both Syria and Iraq.

These threats to the Iraqi water resources have been reinforced by the shaky and unstable relations between Baghdad on one side and Damascus and Ankara on the other side. The Baath party has been in power in both Syrian and Iraq for most of the last three decades. However, the two regimes have since been engaged in a continuous conflict over a variety of issues including their claim of Arab leadership, the peace process with Israel, the conflict in Lebanon, and water-sharing. This large gap in their political orientations as well as the personalistic hostility between the two leaders, Hafez Al Assad and Saddam Hussein, have created and reinforced a sense of mutual suspicion between the two regimes. The tension was escalated in late 1974 and early 1975 when Iraq massed its troops close to the borders with Syria and threatened to bomb the Al Thawra Dam which, according to Baghdad, was reducing the flow of the Euphrates to Iraq. The confrontation ended peacefully thanks to Soviet and Saudi mediations.[58] However, the suspicion and hostility did not stop. Not surprisingly, Syria, unlike the great majority of Arab states, supported Iran in its war against Iraq from 1980 to 1988 and played an active role in the Gulf war in 1991. Meanwhile, Iraq's and Syria's mutual concern over a sufficient and uninterrupted flow of the Euphrates from the upstream riparian, Turkey, has modified their suspicion of each other and provided a common ground where the interests of the two countries coincide. Thus, when Turkey announced in November 1989 that it would stop the flow of the Euphrates for a month (which it did from mid January to mid February 1990) in order to fill the reservoir behind the newly-built Ataturk Dam, delegations

---

[58] Greg Shapland, "Water and Politics in the Middle East," in M. Jane Davis, (ed.), *Politics and International Relations in the Middle East*, Aldershot, UK: Edward Elgar, 1995, p.81.

from Syria and Iraq met and agreed that the former would allow the latter %58 of the flow of the Euphrates at the Turkish-Syrian border.[59] By the second half of the 1990s, Damascus and Baghdad have tried unsuccessfully to coordinate their efforts to block international financing to the Birecik Dam and other Turkish projects on the Euphrates.

Overall, the relations between Baghdad and Ankara have been less tense than those between the former and Damascus. The Turkish and Iraqi interests coincide in many areas particularly in regard to their policy towards the Kurds. For many years the two countries have worked together to fight their Kurdish minorities. Oil is another area of cooperation between the two states. Until the Gulf war, Turkish pipelines were essential for exporting Iraqi oil. Since Baghdad has a very narrow outlet on the Gulf, Iraqi oil was transported to the international market through Saudi and Turkish pipelines in most of the 1980s.[60] Both pipelines were shut down immediately after the Iraqi invasion of Kuwait. In addition to the Kurds and oil, containing the Islamic regime in Tehran has been a mutual concern for both Baghdad and Ankara since 1979.[61]

The Iraqi invasion of Kuwait in August 1990 shattered this spirit of cooperation between Ankara and Baghdad. Thus, Turkish airbases were used during the war to attack Iraq. Equally important, is the fact that these areas of cooperation could not create incentives strong enough to overcome the differences over water sharing. Turkey has always denied any legal obligations to provide water to the downstream riparians. In other words, Turkey emphasizes its adherence to the principle of "absolute territorial sovereignty" which gives Ankara unlimited authority to do whatever it perceives appropriate within its borders. Iraq, on the other side, adheres to the principle of "absolute integrity of a river basin" which limits the right of a unilateral action by an individual riparian and, instead, requests a coordination between all the states which share the basin.[62] The two principles are well-

---

[59] Ibid., p.81.

[60] The Syrian pipelines were shut down early in the 1980s in response to a growing Syrian-Iraqi tension due to the war between the latter and Iran which started in 1980.

[61] The Turkish-Iranian relations had improved tremendously when the Welfare Party was in power in Ankara (1996-1997).

[62] For a discussion of the two theories see Hasan Chalabi and Tarek Majzoub, "Turkey, the Waters of the Euphrates and Public International Law," in J.A. Allan

integrated in the body of the international law. But, Turkey's location as the upstream riparian and its military might (because of its membership in NATO and the destruction of the Iraqi army in the Gulf war) have given Ankara a free hand to implement a number of huge projects on both the Euphrates and the Tigris, which certainly will reduce the flow of the two rivers and will increase their pollution, with little consideration for Baghdad's wishes.

The most well-publicized of these projects is the Great Anatolia Project (GAP). The work on this huge scheme started in 1984 and is expected to take several more years before its completion. It will encompass 20 dams and 17 hydropower plants[63] and will bring under irrigation 1.6 million hectares of land and generate 7,561 megawatts of hydroelectric power.[64] Domestically, the project will transform the underdeveloped south-east Anatolia into a growing agricultural and industrial center. Ankara hopes to solve, or at least alleviate, its problems with its Kurds (who are the majority in the south-east region) by improving their living conditions. Also, the project will empower the Turkish economy by adding these tremendous energy and water resources. Regionally, the GAP will significantly reduce the flow of water from the Euphrates, and to a lesser extent from the Tigris, and will also reduce the quality of water by increasing pollution. Naturally, since the early 1980s, both Syria and Iraq have opposed Turkey's plan. But given their location as downstream riparians and the political and military environment in the region for the last several years, they do not have much leverage to force Ankara to change its policy. Still, it is important to point out that the World Bank has refused to finance the project because of lack of consensus among all the basin-members. By the second half of the 1990s, Turkey has achieved modest success in soliciting Western funds.

---

and Chibli Mallat, (eds.), *Water in the Middle East*, London: I.B. Tauris, 1995, pp.226-228.

[63] Chris Cragg, "Water Resources in the Middle East and North Africa," in *Europa, the Middle East and North Africa 1996*, London: Europa Publications Limited, 1996, p.158.

[64] Thomas Naff, "Hazards to Middle East Stability in the 1990s: Economics, Population, and Water," in Phebe Marr and William Lewis (eds.), *Riding the Tiger*, Boulder: Westview Press, 1993, p.140.

These troubled relations between Iraq and its two neighbors with whom it shares most of its two rivers raise questions regarding the reliability of these sources at present and in the near future. It is worth noting that the three riparian states have failed for several decades to reach an agreement on regulating and sharing the two rivers. In the early 1980s, they created a Technical Committee which lacked any real power and did not pave the road for more cooperation and consultation on water issues. The Gulf war and its aftermath have sharpened Baghdad's sense of vulnerability. The exclusive sanctions imposed on Iraq by the UN following the invasion, have left Baghdad with no other option except self-reliance. The Iraqi government has since doubled its efforts to produce as much food as it can in order to feed its people. This increases Baghdad's needs for fresh water. However, given the political situation, Iraq's growing demands for water have not been answered which adds more incentives for a "water-war" between Baghdad and its neighbors.

This potentiality for a military confrontation over water between Iraq and its partners in the Euphrates basin is offset at least by two factors. On one side, with a little cooperation enough water can be provided for all residents of the three countries. For the time being, there is enough water in the Euphrates-Tigris basin to avert an escalation of a military confrontation. On the other side, Turkey, the upstream riparian, is much more powerful militarily than the two downstream states. This makes the initiation of warfare by Baghdad against Ankara irrational. A more likely scenario is a low-level hostility such as sabotage and terrorism. Iraq might use such methods to exert pressure on Turkey in order to force it to change its water policy. Still this low probability of a large-scale military confrontation over water can not be taken for granted given the Iraqi regime's reputation of miscalculation. In short, in absence of an agreed-on agreement between Iraq and its neighbors on how to share and regulate their water resources, the issue will remain as a potential source of conflict which might explode at any time. To some extent, this conclusion applies in different ways to the water problem in the Gulf monarchies.

WATER SCARCITY IN THE GULF MONARCHIES

The six Arab states are largely desert, have a very arid climate, and receive very little and irregular rainfall.[65] In addition to this low rainfall, the region lacks any reliable surface water. In other words, the sources of fresh water are very limited and there are no prospects for new ones. Because of this severe shortage, water-availability per capita is among the lowest in the world. The region has always lived with the reality of water scarcity, but over the last few decades the problem has become more acute. As has been discussed above, the high population growth rate and economic development have contributed significantly to the rise of demand for fresh water. At the same time, the supply of water has remained constant and even shrunk over the years. The outcome has been a growing imbalance between supply and demand. Simply stated, increasingly the available resources can not satisfy the growing demand.

Given the very low rainfall and the general unavailability of surface runoff, groundwater aquifers are considered the only dependable source of water. They are: the Saq, Tabuk, Wajid, Minjur-Druma, Wasia-Biyadh, Dammam, Um er-Radhuma, Neogene, Aruma, Jauf, Khuff, Jilh, Sakaka, Upper Jurassic, Lower Cretaceous, and Buwaib.[66] It is important to highlight some of the main characteristics of these groundwater aquifers. First, some of them are trans-borders meaning that they are shared by more than one country. Second, the quality of their water varies from one aquifer to another and in some cases is not suitable for human consumption. Third, the recharge rate is very low in most of them. Meanwhile, they suffer from "over-consumption" which suggests that they can be depleted within the next few decades.

This gloomy scenario of water conditions in the Gulf monarchies has been aggravated further by certain economic policies. As will be discussed in more

---

[65] The amount of annual rainfall they receive are as follows, Bahrain: 80 mm, Kuwait: 135 mm, Oman: 71 mm, Qatar: 73, Saudi Arabia: 59, and UAE: 89 mm. See Peter H. Gleick, *A Guide to the World's Fresh Water Resources*, New York: Oxford University Press, 1993, p.141.

[66] Jamil Al Alawi and Muhammad Abdulrazzak, "Water in the Arabian Peninsula: Problems and Perspectives," in Peter Rogers and Peter Lydon, (eds.), *Water in the Arab World: Perspectives and Prognoses*, Cambridge, MA: Harvard University Press, 1994, p.179.

detail shortly, oil prices, after two big rises in 1973 and 1979, have been stagnant at a relatively low level since the mid 1980s. This drop in oil revenues incited Gulf states to consider other sources for national income besides oil. This new attitude is labeled "diversification" and has been promoted with great anxiety. Since the mid 1980s, most of the governments in the region have embarked on a huge public investment in an attempt to diversify their economic structure. The agriculture sector received special attention. The unstable political and security environment in the region since the late 1970s highlighted the fear of a "food-weapon." In other words, special attention was given to the likelihood of blocking food imports by regional or international powers for political reasons. Given the fact that the Gulf monarchies are the largest importers of food per capita in the world,[67] the prospect of a "food-weapon" became a significant national threat. Thus, substantial public funds were allocated to subsidizing domestic food production. The case of Saudi Arabia is a good illustration.

In 1991, the kingdom was a major exporter of heavily subsidized wheat. The Saudi government was not satisfied with achieving self-sufficiency in wheat production, which it could have bought from the global market at a much cheaper price. Instead, the kingdom subsidized exported wheat, produced mainly through irrigated agriculture, which in the final analysis meant exporting water. This policy was abandoned in 1994.[68] Since the mid 1990s, most of the Gulf monarchies have realized that self-sufficiency, particularly in agriculture, is not a realistic goal and that they will always be dependent on imported food because of the unavailability of fresh water resources. By the closing years of the 1990s, a growing concern in water conservation has been on the rise in the Gulf states. Moreover, water has been gradually thought of as a scarce commodity which requires government regulations to guarantee an optimum consumption. In this regard, many solutions have been "considered," others have already been tried. They can be grouped into three categories: improved national management, desalination, and reallocation.

---

[67] Thomas Naff, "Sources of Potential Conflict in the Persian Gulf: The Water Factor," in Geoffrey Kemp and Janice Gross Stein, (eds.), *Powder keg in the Middle East*, Lanham, MD: Rowman and Littlefield Publishers, 1995, p.301.

[68] Edmund O'Sullivan, "Kingdom opts for desalting solutions," *Middle East Economic Digest*, Vol.38, No.4, January 28, 1994, p.9.

First, national management, as has been discussed above, high population growth is a main constraint on water availability. Naturally, a population stabilization should ease the pressure on water resources. Moreover, popular and government awareness of the magnitude of water shortage has just started over the last few years. Consequently, there is severe lack of planning, data collection, qualified personnel, and institutions. Because of this low awareness, water has been provided to consumers either free of charge or heavily subsidized which encourages waste. Market mechanisms and financial incentives need to be introduced in a more aggressive pattern. This should help curbing over-consumption in urban centers. Cutting off subsidies to irrigated agriculture in particular, and to agrarian products in general, should save a significant proportion of the limited water resources given the fact that the agrarian sector consumes far more water than both the industrial and the municipal ones. Finally, more consideration should be given to the utilization of the treatment and re-use of effluent.

Second, desalination: most of the steps discussed above require a long period of time to be implemented and they include a political price. Reducing or cutting off subsidies on such crucial commodity as water can cause popular resentment particularly because it has been provided free of charge for a long time. A less controversial solution is desalination which does not include either creating new institutions or changing public attitude. Thus, the Gulf monarchies account for more than half of the world desalination capacity.[69] Moreover, their dependence on desalinated water from the Gulf has increased in the last few decades. However, two important shortfalls of desalination as a solution to water scarcity in the Gulf are worth discussing. On one side, desalination costs between $1 to $1.5 per cubic meter.[70] With this high price, desalination has been used mainly to satisfy domestic and industrial needs and is still considered too expensive for irrigated agriculture. It is expected that technical innovations would reduce the costs. however, at the end of the 1990s, these expectations have not been realized. On the other side, desalination installations are extremely vulnerable. Relatively speaking, it is easy to attack them by air, missiles, or even by internal sabotage. Many of Kuwaiti desalination installations were destroyed by the Iraqis during the Gulf

---

[69] Peter H. Gleick, *Water in Crisis: A Guide to the World's Fresh Water Resources*, New York: Oxford University Press, 1993, p.422.

[70] Daniel Hillel, *Rivers of Eden*, New York: Oxford University Press, 1994, p.253.

war. These two shortfalls opened the door for a third option to overcome water shortage in the Gulf.

Third, reallocation, the growing imbalance between water supply and demand in the Gulf has aroused the imagination of both policy-makers and scholars to consider solutions which could have been thought unthinkable just few decades ago. Towing icebergs from the Antarctic is a case in point. Another proposal which has been under serious negotiations in the mid 1990s is the transfer of water from the Karoun river in Iran to Qatar through a pipeline. The project faces strong opposition by both Iraq and Saudi Arabia for obvious political reasons.

However, the most publicized scheme is the "Peace Pipeline." In 1987, the then Turkey's Prime Minister Turgut Ozal proposed the construction of two pipelines to carry water from two Turkish rivers: the Seyhan and the Ceyhan. The western pipeline would flow through Syria, Jordan, and terminate in Saudi Arabia. The eastern one would serve Kuwait, eastern Saudi Arabia, Bahrain, Qatar, UAE, and Oman. The American engineering company Brown and Root estimated that cost in 1986 US dollars would be $8.5 billion for the western pipeline and $12.5 for the eastern one.[71] Also, it was estimated that the construction would take approximately 10 years.[72] The Peace Pipeline project was supposed to benefit all the parties. Arab countries would have received badly needed water for as low cost as $0.15 to $0.20[73] (a much lower cost than that of the desalination.) Meanwhile, Turkey would have gained extra cash for its water surplus.

However, in 1991 Ozal lost the elections to Suleiman Demirel and two years later he died. The subsequent Turkish governments have since shown less enthusiasm in the project and have had second thought regarding the availability of a "substantial water surplus." Also on the Arab side there was not much of an interest in the scheme. The fear of dependence on Turkey to satisfy such strategic commodity as water did not appeal to many Arab leaders

---

[71] John Kolars, "Problems of International River Management: The Case of the Euphrates," in Asit K. Biswas, (ed.), *International Waters of the Middle East*, New York: Oxford University Press, 1994, p.78.

[72] Stephen C. McCaffrey, "Water, Politics, and International Law," in Peter H. Gleick, (ed.), *Water in Crisis*, New York: Oxford University Press, 1993, p.94.

[73] J.A. Allan, "Overall Perspectives on Countries and Regions," in Peter Rogers and Peter Lydon, (eds.), *Water in the Arab World*, Cambridge, MA: Harvard University Press, 1994, p.77.

given the fact that in their long history the two sides have not always enjoyed warm relation. In addition, the vulnerability of the long pipelines to sabotage or terrorism was considered. Finally, Israel would have been a possible recipient of water from the western line which, in late 1980s, did not appeal to the Arab leaders. Still, it is worth noting that the Peace Pipeline scheme has not been fully rejected by the Gulf states. A growing water problem can re-activate interest in the project.

To sum up, it is important to re-emphasize that the gap between water demand and supply is getting wider. There is an urgent need to do something to close the gap or at least to stop it from getting larger. The three solutions discussed above include both the supply side (desalination and importation should increase the availability of water) and the demand side (altering the pattern of consumption should reduce the demand.) They complement each other and together can stop, or more likely slow, the aggravation of the water problem in the region.

CONCLUSION

By the last decade of the twentieth century water has become on the agenda in most of the Gulf states. Over the last few years, there has been a growing recognition of the different dimensions of the problem and of the need to solve it. However, the current patterns of consumption need drastic alteration in order to prevent a large-scale water crisis. Meanwhile, the competition over the scarce water resources is getting more intense all across the region. In closing, a few conclusions discussed above need to be re-emphasized. First, since August 1990, Iraq has been forced to take measures to produce all, or most, of its food needs. This has put more pressure on water resources. Moreover, regardless of any changes in the make-up of the political system in Baghdad, the Iraqi requirements for water are expected to increase in order to meet the large-scale reconstruction which is likely to take place immediately after any long-term peace arrangements. This should complicate the relations between Iraq on one side and both Syria and Turkey on the other side. Second, if the recent past is any guide, Iran is not expected to pursue an aggressive hydropolitics against its Gulf neighbors. Water is less important an area of conflict between Tehran and its surrounding states. Other issues such as the Kurds, the Shi'is, oil, and territorial disputes are considered by the two sides more crucial. Also, Tehran shares very little fresh water resources with its Arab neighbors. Third, unlike Iran, Turkey will keep playing a central role in the water and food policies in the region. Given its substantial surplus and ambitious plans, it is hard to imagine any regional water arrangement without Ankara's participation. The recent growing Turkish interest in its Islamic roots and Middle Eastern neighbors increases the potential of finding a common ground between Ankara and the Gulf states. Fourth, the geo-policy of water in the Gulf monarchies does not correspond to the states' boundaries. In other words, the aquifers run through a large area with no consideration to the borders which separate one nation-state from another. This geographical fact strongly suggests that a unilateral solution to the water-shortage is not an option. A regional cooperation is a necessity. Fifth, a large body of the literature on water in the region questions the likelihood of water-induced conflicts in the foreseeable future. However, it is worth noting that Iraq invaded Kuwait in 1990 because of oil, among other things. The increasingly severe water-shortage has added more significance to the water factor in domestic and regional politics. It is to be remembered that unlike oil, water has no substitute. In short, the likelihood of a water-incited military conflict is growing and should not be ruled out.

In summary, water is, and will remain to be, an important source of conflict and/or cooperation in the region. Meanwhile, it is worth emphasizing that water sharing is not a zero-sum game. All participating parties can benefit by coordinating their efforts. The question is which course will the Gulf leaders choose? Only time will tell.

Chapter 3

PEACE IN THE PERSIAN GULF: THE SHI'IS DIMENSION

For several centuries religion has been an important social and political force in the Persian Gulf societies. In addition to national identity, religious and sectarian affiliations have represented significant cleavages within and between the eight Gulf states. The first was introduced by the Western powers mostly in the twentieth century while the other two have dominated the Gulf societies from the very beginning of their existence. Over the centuries, several religious communities have resided in the Persian Gulf region. These include Baha'ai, Christian, Hindu, Ibadhi, Jewish, Muslim, and Zoroastrian religions. The great majority of Gulf residents are Muslims. Within Islam the split between Sunni and Shi'is has important political implications on domestic and regional stability in the region.

Shortly after Prophet Muhammad died, the Islamic community split between two groups: the Sunnis who supported the ascendancy to power of the four "guided" caliphs, and the Shi'is who held that only Ali, the Prophet's cousin and son-in-law, and his descendants should rule the realms of Islam. The first group triumphed and has become the dominant sect in Islam until today. The Shi'is, on the other hand, representing about eleven percent of world Muslims[74], have been in the opposition side for most of the Islamic history. This political marginalization of the Shi'is has been translated into fewer economic and social opportunities in comparison with those available to their Sunni counterparts. Thus, it can be argued that this religious disagreement in the early days of the Islamic state has gained specific socio-

---

[74]Cyril Glasse, The Concise Encyclopedia of Islam, New York: Harper and Row Publishers, 1989, p.364.

economic and political characteristics due to historical experience.[75] Bernard
Lewis, a prominent Islamic historian, describes the difference between the two
sects as follows, "Sunnism is associated with status quo; Shi'ism with a
rejection of status quo, often though not necessarily accompanied by a
determination to change it.[76].

This statement may be an oversimplification since the two sects have
played different roles, for and against the political establishment, in their long
history.[77] Still, it sheds some lights on the fact that Shi'ism has provided some
of the most powerful themes of revolutionary protest in the Islamic world,
including modern day Persian Gulf states. The political map of the region was
drawn, largely, by Britain with little attention to the sectarian identities. Put
differently, the political borders between the eight Gulf states do not necessary
correspond to the sense of group cohesiveness (based on religion, tribe, and
other attributes). This collective religious identity has been maintained by a
common historical experience and through the Shi'i mourning houses (ma'tam
in Bahrain, husayniyya in Kuwait and Saudi Arabia), which function as places
of religious observance and as active family and community centers.[78]

Under the current political conditions in the Gulf, the Shi'is are scattered
all over the region. More than ninety percent of the Iranian population are
Shi'is and the Islamic Republic is the only state in the world where Shi'is are
in power. Iran adopted Shi'ism for several centuries and it has since been an
important socio-economic and political force in the Iranian psychology.
Nevertheless, for many years the Pahlavi regime was able to suppress the Shi'i
opposition. Ayatollah Khomeini's ascendancy to power and the establishment
of the Islamic regime in 1979 opened a new chapter for the Shi'is in Iran with
important implication for the other Gulf states.

---

[75] Bernard Lewis, "Shi'a in Islamic History," in Martin Kramer, (ed.), *Shi'ism,
Resistance, and Revolution*, Boulder, CO: Westview Press, 1987, p.30.

[76] For detailed and massive information on Shi'ism, Shi'i literature and organizations
see the Website on the Internet WWW.Shia.Org.

[77] Several Shi'i dynasties ruled different parts of the Islamic world at various times.
These include the Buyids, Hamdanids, Zaydis, Fatimids, and Safavids. Likewise,
there have been important Sunni movements which have resisted the status quo
such as the Wahhabis in Saudi Arabia, the Mahdist movement in Sudan, and the
Muslim Brotherhood in Egypt.

[78] Fuad Khuri, *Tribe and State in Bahrain*, Chicago: University Press of Chicago,
1980, pp.154-173.

On the Arab side of the Gulf in Bahrain and Iraq, Shi'is are considered "subordinate majorities" (numerically, they are the largest sectarian group but they are not in power.) They represent seventy percent in the former and sixty percent in the latter. In the other Gulf states, Shi'is are "significant minorities.[79]" They are thirty percent in Kuwait, sixteen percent in the UAE, fifteen percent in Qatar, ten percent in Oman, and eight percent in Saudi Arabia.[80]

Two general observations on the distribution of Shi'is in the Gulf states need to be highlighted. First, regardless of the proportion of Shi'is in each state, Shi'ism has been an important issue in both domestic and foreign policies in all of them for many years and is likely to maintain its significance well into the new millennium. Given the sensitivity of sectarianism in the region, the Gulf states have been very reluctant to publish any data on their religious communities. Thus, these figures should be taken with caution and should be seen more as general trends and less as accurate numbers. More certain is the location of the Shi'is in the region. The great majority of them are concentrated next to the rich oil fields and around the shores of the Gulf. In other words, the world's oil heartland also happens to be the Shi'i heartland.[81] This geo-political fact adds significant dimension to the issue of Shi'ism in the Gulf. Simply stated, the security of oil supplies from the region relies, more or less, on the quietness of the Shi'is (either through repression or accommodation.)

This chapter seeks to examine the present conditions of the Shi'is in the Gulf. As has been mentioned above, the Shi'is are in power in Iran. In Oman, Qatar, and the UAE the relations between the Shi'i communities and their respective governments have been, overall, less troubling than in their neighbors. After some tension in the early 1980s, the Kuwaiti government has

---

[79] The two terms "significant minority" and "subordinate majority" are borrowed from Ted Robert Gurr, *Minorities at Risk: A Global View of Ethnopolitical Conflicts*, Washington DC: United States Institute of Peace Press, 1993, pp.3-27.

[80] All the numbers were obtained from the Central Intelligence Agency, *The World Factbook*, Washington DC, United States Government Printing Office, 1998. And Europa Publications, The Middle East and North Africa, London, Europa Publications Limited, 1998.

[81] R.K.Ramazani, "Shi'ism in the Persian Gulf," in Juan R.I. Cole and Nikki R. Keddie, (eds.), *Shi'ism and Social Protest*, New Haven: Yale University Press, 1986, p.30.

succeeded, to a great extent, in accommodating its Shi'i population. The three Gulf states where the Shi'i issue has not been settled down yet are Bahrain, Saudi Arabia, and Iraq. These are the subject of the following analysis. In each case, Shi'ism will be examined not as a religious movement but as a social protest one. The dynamics of the group and the regimes' responses will be addressed. Finally, the study concludes with a prediction of the future of Shi'i communities in the Gulf in the light of domestic, regional, and international developments. An important findings of the following analysis is that a durable peace, which would guarantee the security of oil supplies, requires, among other developments, the peaceful assimilation of the Shi'i communities in their respective states.

SHI'IS IN SAUDI ARABIA

Three important developments have shaped the Shi'i movement in the kingdom in its modern history. These are: the expansion of Wahhabism, the discovery of oil, and the revolution in Iran. Wahhabism is an Islamic movement founded by Muhammad Ibn Abd Al Wahhab in the eighteenth century. The members call themselves muwahhidun "unitarians" and regard themselves Sunnis following the school of Ibn Hanbal. The doctrines of the movement emphasize the belief in tawhid (the oneness of God) and the destruction of all bida (unaccepted innovations.[82]) These principles were endorsed by Muhammad Ibn Saud, the grandfather of King Abd Al Aziz Ibn Saud who founded the modern day Saudi Arabia in 1932. Thus, this alliance between the religious authority (the Wahhabis) and the political one (the Saudis) has endured for more than two centuries. To this day, the legitimacy of Saudi rule has been intimately linked with the religious and social message of Wahhabism.

From the very beginning the Wahhabi conceptual framework has proven intolerant of Shi'i beliefs and practices particularly the veneration of Ali's descendants.[83] This animosity was demonstrated as early as 1801 when

---

[82] M.TH. Houtsma, A.J. Wensinck, H.A.R. Gibb, W. Heffening, and E. Levi-Provencal, (eds.), *The Encyclopedia of Islam*, London: Luzac, 1934, p.1086.

[83] It is also important to point out that Wahhabism opposes other religious practices and philosophies such as Sufism.

Saudi/Wahhabi forces attacked the town of Karbala, sacred to the Shi'is. In the course of the attack, the domes of various tombs-including that of Ali's son, Hussein-were demolished, and the whole city was plundered.[84] More recently, this attitude was re-enforced in a major conference in Riyadh in 1927, which many Saudi and Wahhabi leaders attended. They issued fatwa (binding religious opinion) according to which Shi'i practices were forbidden. In 1991, a similar edict was issued by Ibn Baz, the head of the religious establishment in the kingdom.[85]

To sum up, the doctrines of Wahhabism, a main source of the Saudi political system's legitimacy, completely reject the beliefs and practices of the Shi'is and, consequently, restrict any public display of the Shi'i celebrations and worship. These religious disparities were further aggravated by the discovery of oil which added socio-economic grievances to the already large gap separating the two sides.

In 1933, a concession was granted to Standard Oil Company of California to explore for oil in Saudi Arabia. The operating company, the Arabian-American Oil Company (ARAMCO) began exploration in that year and discovered oil in commercial quantities in 1938.[86] The massive production began shortly after the Second World War and the expansion of the Saudi Arabia's oil output in the subsequent decades has been spectacular. Ironically, most of the largest oil fields in the kingdom, and in the world, such as Ghawar are located in the Eastern Province where Shi'is constitute about 33 percent of the population.[87] This heavy Shi'i concentration added to their alienation. The perception among at least some of the Shi'i residents was that the country's main source of revenue is located in their heartland, however, they have been suppressed and denied many of the social services and economic benefits provided to their Sunni counterparts.

---

[84] Jacob Goldberg, "The Shi'i Minority in Saudi Arabia," in Juan R.I. Cole and Nikki R. Keddie, (eds.), *Shi'ism and Social Protest*, New Haven: Yale University Press, 1986, p.232.

[85] Madawi Al Rasheed and Loulouwa Al Rasheed, "The Politics of Encapsulation: Saudi Policy towards Tribal and Religious Opposition," *Middle Eastern Studies*, Vol.32, No.1, January 1996, p.110.

[86] Europa Publications, The Middle East and North Africa, London: Europa Publications Limited, p.868.

[87] Helen Chapin Metz, (ed.), *Saudi Arabia: A Country Study*, Washington DC: United States Government Printing Office, 1993, p.85.

At the same time, due to regional and international developments, oil prices skyrocketed. In 1960, oil revenues were $400 million, a decade later they reached $1.2 billion[88], and by 1980 they jumped to the unprecedented peak of $99 billion.[89] This unbelievable wealth created a special economic and political system known as "rentierism[90]" and enabled the government to embark on an ambitious development plan. This included huge spending on socio-economic infrastructure such as paving new roads, building new schools and hospitals, expanding the bureaucracy and creating a bigger and better-equipped armed forces. However, the financial resources allocated to the Eastern Province, where the Shi'is are concentrated, were much lower than public spending in the rest of the country. This disparity aggravated the Shi'is' sense of discrimination and their perception of inequality. Under these circumstances, a sense of Shi'i identity was growing and gained momentum by the triumph of the Islamic revolution in the neighboring Iran in the early 1979.

It is important to emphasize from the outset that the resentments expressed by some Shi'is toward their government are born, primarily, in response to perceived religious discrimination which produces inferior socioeconomic and political status. In other words, the marginalization of the Shi'is in the public sphere provides a strong explanation to their opposition to the political system. This has happened, and will continue to happen, regardless of any support they might receive from the outside. At the same time, it is also true that Khomeini's success in overthrowing the Pahlavi regime provided the Shi'is in Saudi Arabia and elsewhere with a sense of self-confidence and a source of inspiration. Not surprisingly, two important riots took place in the Eastern Province shortly after the Iranian revolution.

Reflecting a new spirit of assertiveness and in defiance of public authority, Shi'i leaders announced in late November 1979 that they would

---

[88] Keith McLachlan, "Oil in the Persian Gulf Area," in Alvin J. Cottrell, (ed.), *The Persian Gulf States*, Baltimore: The Johns Hopkins University Press, 1980, p.218.

[89] Central Intelligence Agency, *Handbook of International Economic Statistics*, Washington DC: United States Government Publication Office, 1995, p.94.

[90] A rentier state derives a substantial part of its revenue selling one or few products. See Hazem Beblawi and Giacomo Luciani, (eds.), *The Rentier State*, London: Croom Helm, 1987, p.11.

publicly stage the Ashura ceremony.[91] The celebration quickly turned into violent clashes with the security forces stationed in the area. Two months later, on the first anniversary of Khomeini's ascendance to power, a similar riot occurred and was suppressed, once again, by the National Guard. It is important to point out that in the two events the demonstrators demanded more freedom to practice their rituals in public and bigger share in the, then, expanding economic pie. To put it differently, they wanted the religious discrimination to be lifted and demanded more opportunities in jobs, education, and public housing. The government reacted by employing a carrot and stick approach. The first step was a wave of arrest which included hundreds of people who participated in the riots. This was followed by an increase in public spending in an attempt to improve the social and economic infrastructure in the Eastern Province. In addition, many high-ranking public officials, including King Khalid, visited the region to demonstrate the government's concern. This combination of punishment and reward seems to have succeeded in reducing incentives for violence in the remaining of the 1980s. Furthermore, in the early 1990s, when Sunni opposition to the royal family was on the rise, the Saudi government invested more efforts to accommodate the Shi'i demands. Accordingly, some of the Shi'i leaders in exile were invited to return to the kingdom. Furthermore, the King appointed prominent Shi'is in the Consultative Council in 1993 and 1997.[92] In response, the Reform Movement, a Shi'i opposition group based in London, suspended its attack on the Saudi regime. Nevertheless, this rapprochement did not last for long. The Al Khobar attack in June 1996 which killed nineteen US military personnel and injured hundreds others, was followed by a campaign of arrest and detention of suspected opposition activists particularly among the Shi'is. According to the Human Rights Watch, twenty-three Shi'i clerics and religious scholars were among the hundreds who were arrested shortly after

---

[91] The holy day of Ashura, commemorating the martyrdom in battle of the third Shi'i imam, Hussein, is the most solemn in the Shi'i calendar and the emotive peak of a major religious period observed by the Shi'is-the month of Muharram.

[92] R. Hrair Dekmejian, "Saudi Arabia's Consultative Council," *Middle East Journal*, Vol.52, No.2, Spring 1998, p.213.

the attack. [93] These violent confrontations between the Shi'is and the Saudi government were echoed in the neighboring Bahrain.

SHI'IS IN BAHRAIN

In the recent years, Bahrain has experienced more political violence than most of its Gulf neighbors. The opposition groups behind this unrest are predominantly, but not exclusively, Shi'i. This persistent confrontation between the government and its opponents can be explained by the three unique geo-political and historical characteristics of the archipelago: oil, Shi'i majority ruled by a Sunni royal family, and extensive Iranian influence. First, Bahrain was the first state on the Arabian side of the Gulf to produce oil. In the first half of the 1930s oil, in commercial quantity, was discovered and exported. [94] These accesses to oil wealth earlier than most of the other Gulf states provided Manama with the means to initiate social and economic development. However, unlike other states in the Gulf such as Saudi Arabia, Kuwait and Iraq, Bahraini oil reserves are very limited and its current fields are almost depleted. In the near future, Bahrain will be the first Gulf state to experience a future without oil. The diminishing revenues have slowed down economic prosperity, fueled social problems and reduced the government's ability to buy off its opponents. Second, the suffering from these stagnant socio-economic conditions have not been shared equally between the different segments in the population. The Shi'is have paid higher price than their Sunni counterparts. This inequality can be explained partly by the fact that Bahrain is the only Gulf state with a Shi'i majority who are ruled by a Sunni royal family. Given these conditions, some Shi'is claim that there is discrimination in jobs, education, housing, and public spending in favor of the Sunni minority. Observers from international human rights organizations have recently substantiated these claims. [95] Third, Iran-the most populous Gulf state-

---

[93] *Human Rights Watch, Human Rights Watch World Report* 1997, New York: Human Rights Watch, 1996, p.298.

[94] Richard F. Nyrop, (ed.), *Area Handbook for the Persian Gulf States*, Washington DC: United States Government Printing Office, 1977, p.207.

[95] For example, see Joe Stork, *Routine Abuse, Routine Denial: Civil Rights and the Political Crisis in Bahrain*, New York: Human Rights Watch, 1997.

has, at different times, made historical claims over the whole archipelago. These claims are based on the fact that seventy percent of the Bahraini population are Shi'i, eight percent of them are ethnically Iranians[96] and, finally, the emirate was ruled by Persia (the ancient name of Iran) for a long time. These claims were reactivated in the first few months after the Iranian revolution.

Given these characteristics, the history of Bahrain since its independence in 1971 has been dominated by political unrest between the opposition, mostly Shi'i, and the royal family. The elected legislature in 1973 had a Shi'i majority and was dissolved by the Emir only two years after its inception. It has been replaced by an appointed Consultative Council with very limited power.[97] The revival of the elected Assembly has since been a main goal for the opposition. Like in Saudi Arabia, the Islamic revolution in Iran provided the Shi'is in Bahrain with a sense of self-confidence. One of the earliest manifestations of this spirit was in 1980 when huge demonstrations were orchestrated against the Iraqi embassy in Manama when the regime in Baghdad arrested, and later executed, Ayatollah Sayyid Muhammad Baqir Al Sadr, a prominent Shi'i cleric, and his sister Bint Al Huda.

More serious was an alleged Iranian-supported coup plot in December 1981. According to the government in Manama, more than seventy people were arrested and charged of planning to assassinate Bahraini officials.[98] Claims were made that they were trained in and supported by Iran which categorically denied these accusations. A similar episode occurred about fifteen years later in June 1996 when the government of Bahrain announced the arrest of 29 Bahraini suspects in connection with a purported Iranian-backed plot to overthrow the ruling family and replace it with a Shi'i regime.[99] Again, Tehran rejected these claims.

In addition to blaming Iran for its internal problems, the government of Bahrain has pursued four more strategies in order to contain the Shi'i uprising.

---

[96] Central Intelligence Agency, *The World Factbook*, Washington DC: United States Government Printing Office, 1995, p.33.

[97] For more details see Rosemarie Said Zahlan, *The Making Of The Modern Gulf States: Kuwait, Bahrain, Qatar, The United Arab Emirates And Oman*, London: Unwin Hyman, 1989, particularly chapter 4, pp.46-65.

[98] Facts On File, December 25, 1981, p.949.

[99] Facts On File, June 13, 1996, p.406.

First, the authorities in Manama have not hesitated to employ coercive methods including execution.[100] The government utilized the 1974 State Security Act which permits it to detain individuals accused of anti-government activity for up to three years without a trial.[101] Thus, Waves of arrest and detention characterize the government response to the Shi'i upheavals. These included prominent popular leaders such as Ali Salman and Abd Al Amir Al Jamri. Second, the government sought assistance from conservative Arab and Muslim countries particularly Saudi Arabia. In 1995, it was reported that some 4,000 Saudi security officers were dispatched to reinforce the Bahraini police.[102] This cooperation was in line with a joint security pact signed between the two countries in December 1981.[103] Furthermore, Riyadh decided to allocate its share of output from the Abu Safa oilfield to Bahrain. Third, some changes in the political system were introduced by the government and presented as genuine steps toward national unity and popular participation, but were perceived by most of the opposition groups as cosmetic. For example, the first major cabinet reshuffle in nearly two decades was announced in mid 1995. However, there were no changes in the main portfolios (defense, interior, foreign affairs, and economy.) In the same year, the government initiated talks with the Shi'i leaders but in few months these negotiations collapsed. In addition, the Emir offered to expand the membership of the government-appointed Consultative Council from 30 to 40 and to allow up to one-half of the members to be elected indirectly through professional and cultural organizations. Fourth, the government has sought to expand its control over all religious institutions particularly the Shi'i mosques and other civil associations. In April 1996, a decree was announced creating a Higher Council of Islamic Affairs which will be responsible for screening nominations for Shi'i clerics. Moreover, the incomes and expenditures of the mosques will be under the control of the Council. Finally, the Council will

---

[100] In March 1996, the first official execution since 1977 was carried out against Ahmed Hassan Qambar, a Shi'i dissident.

[101] Roger Kaplan, (ed.), *Freedom in the World*, New York: Freedom House, 1996, p.132.

[102] *Europa Publications, The Middle East and North Africa*, London: Europa Publications Institution, 1996, p.319.

[103] Facts On File, December 25, 1981, p.949.

distribute scholarships among theology students and the government will undertake to find jobs for them.[104]

It is still to early to make any judgment on how effective these strategies in curbing the Shi'i opposition. Rather, it can be argued, with some certainty, that the socio-economic and political grievances of the Shi'is need to be addressed in order to achieve domestic stability. This conclusion can be equally applied to the neighboring Iraq.

SHI'IS IN IRAQ

As has been indicated above, the Shi'is represent the majority of the Iraqi population. Besides this numerical advantage, some Iraqi cities such as Karbala, Najaf, and Kazimayn contain shrines of special significance in Shi'i theology and history. Currently, these cities are centers of learning and attract Shi'i pilgrims from all over the world.[105] Given this significance of Shi'ism in Iraq, it is astonishing that the Shi'is have never enjoyed economic benefits and political rights equal to their Arab Sunni counterparts (about fifteen percent of the population[106]) who have dominated the political system in Baghdad since its independence from Britain in 1932. Leaving aside a small number of wealthy business executives and professionals, most Iraqi Shi'is form an impoverished underclass in Baghdad and southern Iraq suffering from widespread discrimination and oppression.[107] Their conditions have further deteriorated since the collapse of the monarchy in 1958 and more specifically since the Baath party returned to power in 1968. The central role of secularism and Arab unity in the Baath's ideology does not appeal to some of the Iraqi Shi'is. Furthermore, the party's insistence on expanding its control over all aspects of life naturally collided with the clerics' authority over the religious

---

[104] Louay Bahry, "The Opposition in Bahrain: A Bellwether for the Gulf?" *Middle East Policy*, Vol.5, No.2, May 1997, p.54.

[105] Elie kedourie, "The Iraqi Shi'is and their fate," in Martin Kramer, (ed.), *Shi'ism, Resistance, and Revolution*, Boulder, CO: Westview Press, 1987, p.136.

[106] Helen Chapin Metz, (ed.), *Iraq: A Country Study*, Washington DC: United States Government Printing Office, 1990, p.81.

[107] Andrew Whitley, "Minorities and the Stateless in Persian Gulf Politics," *Survival*, Vol.35, No.4, Winter 1993, p.36.

institutions. Thus, for many years, the relationship between the Shi'i majority
and the Baath party has been characterized by suspicion, confrontation, and
overall uneasiness.

The Gulf war and its aftermath were perceived, for a short time, as a
"window of opportunity" for the Shi'is to acquire a bigger share of the political
power in Baghdad. The international coalition dealt a heavy blow to Saddam's
regime, but not a fatal one. In other words, the Iraqi military capability and
economic infrastructure were severely damaged, but the political structure and
the security apparatus remained intact. This became apparent in the regime's
response to the eruption of the Shi'i rebellion. Shortly after the war, the Shi'i
community in the south, with support from Muhammad Baqir Al Hakim the
head of the Supreme Assembly of the Islamic Republic of Iraq, revolted
against the government. The fighting was most intense in the Shi'i holy cities
of Najaf and Karbala as well as in Basra, the second largest city in Iraq.[108] In
about two weeks, troops loyal to the regime were able to crush the rebellion.
An important reason for the collapse of the Shi'i resistance was the switch in
the American stance in regard to the most appropriate way to overthrow
Saddam Hussein's regime. At the end of the war, President Bush called on the
Iraqi opposition to "rise up and throw out the dictator.[109]" This was understood
by the Shi'is (and the kurds) as a promise of military and political support for
their revolt. At the end, they only received humanitarian assistance. Since
then, the Shi'i resistance has been on the wane. At least four developments
have contributed to this gradual decline.

First, the Shi'i community is, to some extent, integrated in the Iraqi state
culturally, economically, and politically, albeit as a junior partner. The lack of
geographical constraints, such as rivers and mountains, between the highly-
concentrated Shi'i regions and the rest of the country has enhanced this
integration. The large Shi'i population in Baghdad can be seen as a
manifestation of the growing interaction between the Sunni and the Shi'i Iraqi
communities. Another case in point is the fact that the great majority of the

---

[108] For a detailed description of the uprising see Faleh Abd Al Jabbar, "Why the
Uprisings," *Middle East Report*, No.176, May-June 1992, pp.2-14.

[109] Quoted in Thomas McNaugher, "Arms Sales and Arms Embargoes in the Persian
Gulf: The Real Dilemmas of Dual Containment," in Geoffrey Kemp and Janice
Gross Stein, (eds.), *Powder Keg in the Middle East*, Lanham, MD: Rowman and
Littlefield Publishers, 1995, p.338.

Shi'is participated in the war against their coreligionists in Iran. Fear of the Baath's brutality was one reason, another was that some Shi'is gave priority to protecting the mother land over defending the faith. It is impossible to know which factor was more crucial, but it is safe to assume that both of them existed and played a role. Finally, it is important to point out that the great majority of the Iraqi Shi'is do not advocate the break up of the country. Unlike the Kurds, the Shi'is' struggle is not for autonomy or self-rule. Rather, they want a fairer distribution of the political and economic resources.

Second, partly as a result of this integration, overall the Shi'i community has not produced any cohesive and strong opposition organization. The supreme Assembly of the Islamic Republic of Iraq established in 1982 under the leadership of Muhammad Baqir Al Hakim, and the Islamic Call party created by the late Ayatollah Muhammad Baqir Al Sadr in 1968 are among the most prominent Shi'i opposition organizations.[110] However, most of these groups, as other non-Shi'i opposition ones, are located outside Iraq, in Tehran, Damascus, London, and elsewhere because of fear of the Baath's brutality. This fact has contributed to their weakness by reducing their ability to establish contact with their constituencies. This has weakened their appeal to the public and made it easier for the government to portray them as agents of foreign powers.

A third reason for the decline of the Shi'i threat in Baghdad is the regime's brutal repression to its opponents. Over the years Iraqi leaders, particularly Saddam Hussein, have not hesitated to use whatever means, regardless of their harshness, to impose their rule. In addition to the execution of many of the Shi'i leaders, in 1980 Saddam Hussein expelled 15,386 Iranian nationals who descended from families that had been living in Iraq for many generations.[111] The official repression against the Shi'is reached its peak in the 1991 uprising. A recent episode which received worldwide attention because of its unprecedented magnitude took place in the Marshlands of southern Iraq. About half a million people, mostly Shi'i, had their own distinctive civilization

---

[110] Amatzia Baram, "The Future of Ba'thist Iraq: Power Structure, Challenges, and Prospects," in Robert B. Satloff, (ed.), *The Politics of Change in the Middle East*, Boulder: Westview Press, 1993, p.48.

[111] Hanna Batatu, "Shi'i Organizations in Iraq: Al-Da'wah Al-Islamiyah and Al-Mujahidin," in Juan R.I. Cole and Nikki R. Keddie, (eds.), *Shi'ism and Social Protest*, New Haven: Yale University Press, 1986, p.196.

for thousands of years. The region was seen by many as the base for, and symbol of, Shi'i resistance.[112] Since 1992, the Iraqi government has embarked on a large-scale project to drain and divert water from the region and, in the process, destroyed this ancient civilization. Allegations were made that the Iraqi regime used chemical weapons and poisoned the water to force the residents out of the region.[113] In October 1996, the government announced the completion of this huge project.[114]

Fourth, another reason for the fading of the Shi'i resistance can be found in the relative lack of international interest in the Shi'i community. The close link between the Iraqi Shi'is and their coreligionists in Iran has prompted the suspicion of regional and international powers. Simply stated, they do not want to see Tehran's influence expands further to southern Iraq. This partly explains the reluctance and hesitation of Western powers to provide the Shi'is in the south with the same level of protection that has been given to the Kurds in the north. Simultaneously, the two communities rebelled against Saddam's regime and were ruthlessly suppressed early in 1991. It took Western powers an additional year to establish a security system for the Shi'is. Meanwhile, the "no-fly" zone in the south has proven far less a constraint on Saddam's brutality than the "safe-haven" zone in the north.[115] In other words, international protection for the Iraqi Shi'is was too little and too late. This gave an opportunity for the regime to further tighten its control over the Shi'i community. Finally, it is worth noting that the Iranian support to the Iraqi Shi'is was neither forthcoming nor unlimited. The Iranian leaders understood that a pro-Tehran regime in either south Iraq or in Baghdad would not be permitted by regional and international powers. The maximum the Islamic Republic could achieve was to use its cordial and extensive connections with the Iraqi Shi'is to expand its influence in the Gulf region. Thus, Tehran has hosted a number of Iraqi opposition groups and provided them with some

---

[112] Ofra Bengio, "The Challenge to the Territorial Integrity of Iraq," *Survival*, Vol.37, No.2, Summer 1995, p.87.

[113] International Institute for Strategic Studies, Strategic Survey, London: *Brassey's*, 1994, p.140.

[114] *Middle East Economic Digest*, "Iraq: An Ambitious Scheme in an Afflicted Land," Vol.40, No.43, October 25, 1996, p.26.

[115] The no-fly zone was expanded from the 32 parallel to the 33 one in September 1996.

assistance, but it has not sought to play a leading role in ousting the regime in Baghdad.

CONCLUSION: THE GULF SHI'IS IN THE NEW MILLENNIUM

The contention of this study is that a durable and comprehensive peace in the Persian Gulf has an internal and external dimensions. The stunning victory of the international alliance in the Gulf war has reduced the possibility of another inter-state military confrontation. In other words, the heavy Western military presence in the region since the early 1990s, has tremendously diminished the likelihood of another conventional war between regional powers. This relative lack of external threat has shifted the attention to the internal dimension of comprehensive peace (e.g. creating a political consensus by the peaceful assimilation of all socio-economic and political groups.)

An important conclusion of the foregoing analysis is that the status of the Shi'i communities in the Arab Gulf states should be approached less as a "religious" issue and more as a "socio-economic" phenomenon. A fundamental reason for the Shi'i unrest has been the perception of at least some Shi'is that they have been denied a fair share of the economic and political resources in their societies because of their sectarian affiliation. There will be neither long-term domestic stability nor durable regional peace without addressing these grievances.[116] In addition, the future of the Shi'i movements in the Gulf will be shaped by the following developments:

First, the organizational structure of the Shi'i groups in the three case studies is still in the infancy stage. No well-developed organization capable of challenging the ruling authorities has been established yet. This has been aggravated even further by the failure to generate strong charismatic leaders who can appeal to the masses and unite the demands for a re-distribution of political power and a re-slicing of the economic pie. In short, the Shi'i opposition still has a long way to go in order to pose a serious threat to the current ruling regimes. Second, this apparent weakness of the Shi'is should not be over-estimated. They still have the resources to disturb public order. For the last several decades, the royal families in the Gulf and the Baath party in

---

[116] For a similar conclusion see James A. Bill, "Resurgent Islam in the Persian Gulf," *Foreign Affairs*, Vol.63, No.1, Fall 1984, pp.108-127.

Baghdad have employed coercive methods to assimilate their Shi'i communities. With the partial exception of Kuwait, no long-term genuine efforts have been made to address their grievances. Force has succeeded to contain the Shi'i anger temporary, but a deep-rooted stability requires much more than mere coercion. Third, Iran as a major Gulf state and as the only country in the world where Shi'is are in power has the capability to influence the sectarian struggle in the Arab Gulf states. However, more important than the question of "capability" is that of "political will." As has been suggested, the Islamic revolution has provided an inspiration and a momentum to the Shi'i movements in many countries particularly in the beginning. However, when the euphoria started fading, the rhetoric of Iran has become louder than its deed. Slowly, pragmatism has been replacing messianic Islamism as the main motive for Tehran's regional policy. Bluntly, Iran is increasingly more interested in improving relations with its neighbors than in exporting its revolution. This approach is likely to continue under the Khatami's administration as has been illustrated in the gathering of 55 delegations from the Islamic Conference Organization in Tehran in December 1997 and the restoration of diplomatic relations between the Islamic Republic and Bahrain in the same year. Fourth, a re-distribution of the political power between different segments within the Gulf societies would lead to a period of instability. Global powers, almost with no exception, have extensive economic and strategic ties with the royal families in the Gulf and common interest in maintaining the territorial integrity of Iraq. Consequently, the international community has shown very little interest, if any, in supporting any change in the status quo in the region.

The policies of the indigenous Shi'i movements, the ruling elites, Iran, and the global powers would shape the future of the relations between the Shi'is and the Sunnis in the region. An orchestrated efforts need to be made in order to address the socio-economic inequality between the two communities. This would facilitate their peaceful assimilation in the society and would, eventually, contribute to a long-term political stability and lay the foundations for a durable peace.

Chapter 4

THE GULF MONARCHIES: EDUCATION, UNEMPLOYMENT, AND THE GENDER GAP

Since the end of World War II, the global economy has grown dependent on oil supplies from the Persian Gulf. Given the immense reserves in the region, this dependence is likely to increase. The Gulf War of 1991 showed the uncompromising world determination to guarantee the safety of oil fields and shipments. A heavy Western, particularly American, military presence in the region since the Gulf War, has served as a deterrent against any threat to the security of the six Gulf monarchies: Bahrain; Kuwait; Oman; Qatar; Saudi Arabia; and the United Arab Emirates (UAE). This alliance, formal and informal, between the Gulf regimes and the Western powers has reduced tremendously the likelihood of another full-scale war similar to the Iraqi invasion of Kuwait. This relative security from an outside enemy does not, however, eliminate other sources of threat to regional oil supplies.

For the last several years, there have been signs of growing internal instability in a number of the Gulf monarchies. The domestic environment reflects a fundamental structural imbalance between economic growth on the one hand and social and political developments on the other hand. The former has surpassed the latter. Due to the huge oil revenues, Gulf citizens have enjoyed a substantial improvement in their standard of living. Meanwhile, social attitudes and political structures have changed at a much slower pace. This imbalance in the speed of change challenges the stability of the region. Increasingly, the six Gulf regimes have been unable to peacefully assimilate the growing number of emerging social forces, particularly educated youths, into existing economic and political structure.

This chapter focuses on the internal challenges facing the six Gulf monarchies, particularly in managing the influence of education on social mobilization. For the foreseeable future the stability of the six states and the security of oil supplies from the region will be endangered more from within and less from without. The following sections examine imbalances between the educational system and the labor market, between technical training and "academic" studies, between religious and secular education, and between men's and women's participation rates in schooling and employment. In addition, the social, economic and political implications of these mismatches will be analyzed. But first, a discussion of the evolution of the educational system in the Gulf monarchies is in order.

EDUCATION AS AN OBJECT AND AN AGENT OF CHANGE

Unlike other issues, such as economic development or the security of the region, education has received much less attention than it deserves. The Gulf monarchies' success in introducing formal education to their populations is impressive, particularly when compared with their levels of education a generation ago. For example, in 1950, 97.5 percent of Saudi Arabia's population was illiterate.[117]. In 1995, the percentage dropped to 37.2 percent.[118] As table I indicates, similar results were achieved in the other Gulf states.

This high literacy rate, in comparison to that of other Middle Eastern countries, can be explained by one factor: oil. In most of the Gulf monarchies, oil was discovered in commercial quantities shortly after the end of World War II. Oil revenues have provided the financial means to initiate and pursue this stunning expansion in education. In addition to eliminating illiteracy, oil revenues provided the resources to establish institutions of higher education, as table II shows.

---

[117]Bruce M. Russett, *World Handbook of Political and Social Indicators*, New Haven: Yale University Press, 1964, p.224

[118] UNESCO, *Statistical Yearbook*, Lanham, MD: Bernan Press, 1997, p.29.

Table I
Illiteracy Rates in the Gulf Monarchies in 1995

Country	Total	Male	Female
Bahrain	14.8	10.9	20.6
Kuwait	21.4	17.8	25.1
Oman	65.0	N/A	*N/A
Qatar	20.6	20.8	20.1
S. Arabia	37.2	28.5	49.8
UAE	20.8	21.1	20.2

* Data not available

Sources: UNESCO, *Statistical Yearbook*, Lanham, MD: Bernan Press, 1997, pp.23-32; United Nations Development Program, *Human Development Report 1997*, New York: Oxford University Press, 1997, p.147.

Table II
Universities in the Gulf Monarchies in 1996

University	Founded	Teachers	Students
Arab Gulf Univ.	1980	68	368
Univ. of Bahrain	1986	320	6,760
Kuwait Univ.	1962	918	17,447
Sultan Qaboos Univ.	1985	425	5,000
Univ. of Qatar	1973	637	7,794
Muhammad Ibn Saud	1953	1,663	6,270
Islamic Univ.	1961	620	3,140
King Abd Al-Aziz Univ.	1967	1,145	30,773
King Fahd Univ.	1963	806	7,602
King Faisal Univ.	1975	519	4,579
King Saud Univ.	1957	2,768	37,324
Umm Al-Qura Univ.	1981	90	2,000

Source: Europa Publications, *The World of Learning* 1998, Forty-eighth Edition, London: Unwin Brothers Limited, 1996.

The expansion of university-level education in the last few decades demonstrates Gulf rulers' attitudes toward investing in human resources in order to secure a better future for their citizens. In line with this policy, education is provided free of charge at all levels. In addition to no tuition fees, states also provide all necessary textbooks and equipment. The education budget has remained high since commercial oil production began, second only to defense expenditures in most of the Gulf monarchies.[119] Finally, in order to fully appreciate this progress in education, it is important to note that modern education was introduced in the region much later than in the neighboring countries of Iran, Iraq, Syria and Jordan.

The traditional educational system was based on the Kuttab, small religious classes, in which groups of boys or girls were taught to recite the Qur'an, and sometimes taught basic writing and arithmetic. Mosques, and occasionally private homes, served as the location for Kuttab learning. Modernization and increasing integration into the international system have introduced change. The Arabian American Oil Company (ARAMCO) participated in promoting education in Saudi Arabia's eastern province and in 1953 Britain built the first school offering a comprehensive curriculum in Sharjah, UAE.[120] This modern education has not, however, replaced the old religious one. Rather, both educational systems, modern/secular and traditional/religious, co-exist and cause economic and political tensions.

RELIGIOUS EDUCATION AND POLITICAL OPPOSITION

The predominance of religion in most aspects of the educational system is an important characteristic of Gulf societies. Islamic and Arabic studies continue to dominate school and college curricula. The establishment of several universities in the region was meant, at least partly, to reduce the number of students sent to study abroad for fear that they might be influenced by Western culture. Many schools and universities have a strict policy of

---

[119] In the 1997 budget in Saudi Arabia, education represented 23 percent of the total government spending. *Middle East Economic Digest*, "Special Report: Saudi Arabia," Vol.41, No.12, March 21, 1997, p.19.

[120] Helen Chapin Metz, (ed.), *Persian Gulf States: Country Studies*, Washington DC: United States Government Printing Office, 1994, p.210.

gender segregation.[121] This official endorsement of religious education, as well as the impact of the latter on the political process, needs to be addressed.

For several decades, Gulf regimes have been enthusiastic about the expansion of Islamic studies. A number of political developments can explain this official attitude. First, in order to co-opt the traditional Islamic establishment, the six Gulf states have spent generously to build new religious schools and universities. This policy has consolidated the partnership between the leaders of the religious hierarchy and the royal families, particularly in Saudi Arabia. Second, the kingdom and other Gulf states have sought to expand their cultural and political influence in many parts of the Islamic world. A large number of graduates from religious institutions makes achieving this goal possible. Finally, highlighting the pious character of the state has served as a bulwark against both radical Arabism and Iranian fundamentalism.

Ironically, these Islamic institutions have become a two-edged political instrument, serving both as a primary medium of self-legitimation and as the main venue of protest for opposition elements.[122] The same schools and universities which were founded by the governments to enhance and promote their religious image have provided economic and ideological incentives for anti-regime activities. For a long time, the graduates of these schools were recruited into the civil service as preachers or sent abroad on religious missions. The increasing inefficiency of the bureaucracy, as well as the growing number of religious school graduates, has made it harder for the governments to provide them with sufficient employment. Furthermore, the fact that many graduates lack technical training makes it difficult for them to find employment outside the public sector. Accordingly, some remain unemployed for long periods of time and become easy targets for extremist movements and ideas. Finally, the expansion of formal religious education programs in technologically modernizing societies has created some economic

---

[121] In July 1996, the Kuwaiti parliament voted to segregate Kuwait University within five years. See Mary Ann Tetreault, "Designer Democracy in Kuwait," *Current History*, Vol.96, No.606, January 1997, p.37.

[122] R. Hrair Dekmejian, "The Rise of Political Islamism in Saudi Arabia," *Middle East Journal*, Vol.48, No.4, Fall 1994, p.627.

dislocation between those equipped primarily with a religious education and those prepared to work in the modern economic sector.[123]

VOCATIONAL EDUCATION AND THE
UNDER-UTILIZATION OF MANPOWER

Many developing countries suffer from capital shortage and labor abundance. By contrast, the Gulf monarchies experience surpluses of financial resources but lack appropriately trained manpower. This unusual characteristic can be seen as the main reason for the imbalance in the educational system and the mismatch in the labor force.

In all six Gulf states, humanities and social sciences dominate the curriculum at the expense of hard sciences. Traditionally, technical education has been associated with the lower classes. The great majority of the population values "academic" learning more than vocational training. The majority of students choose the less demanding humanities and social sciences in part because the language used for instruction and in the textbooks is usually Arabic. Only a small minority of students elect to study engineering and sciences where the teaching language and materials are often in English and many of the professors are foreign.[124] This tendency among students not to choose vocational training had been reinforced until recently, by the availability of more attractive job opportunities in the civil service. The predominance of humanities in the Gulf states' educational systems is due to insufficient attention to labor-market requirements on the part of policy makers. Decisions to expand education have been made in response to the availability of capital surpluses and not in conjunction with long-term and well-defined national policy. The educational imbalance has caused a distortion of the supply-side of the labor market.

A high level of unemployment among the national labor force is paradoxically accompanied by the presence of a huge number of expatriates. In 1995, foreign workers represented more than 80 percent of the labor force

---

[123] Helen Chapin Metz, *Saudi Arabia: A Country Study*, Washington DC: United States Government Printing Office, 1993, p.104.

[124]Mordechai Abir, *Saudi Arabia in the Oil Era*, Boulder, CO: Westview Press, 1988, p.46.

in the United Arab Emirates and constituted the majority in other states such as Qatar and Kuwait.[125] This can be explained by the gap between the academic education many nationals have received and the technical training their modernizing societies need. The great majority of nationals are employed by their governments, it is estimated that more than 90 percent of Kuwaiti, Saudi, and other Gulf employees work for the public sector.[126] The private sector relies heavily on foreign labor.[127]

The "oil boom" of the 1970s explains this asymmetrical distribution of employees between the private and public sectors. The immense revenues Gulf states received after the huge jump in oil prices incited them to initiate ambitious social and economic plans. Given their small populations and lack of indigenous trained labor, they invited expatriates to build a state of the art economic infrastructure. Expansion of the education system was designed to prepare nationals to replace foreign workers in developing industries. At the same time, Gulf bureaucracies expanded partly to secure governmental control over the economic, social and political lives of their citizens and partly to provide job opportunities for the increasing number of graduates. This policy of guaranteeing public sector employment to all graduates produced inflated and inefficient bureaucracies, and an under-utilized labor force.

---

[125] Central Intelligence Agency, *The World Factbook*, Washington DC: united States Government Printing Office, 1998.

[126] James Yahya Sadowski, "Prospects for Democracy in the Middle East: The Case of Kuwait," The Fletcher Forum of World Affairs, Vol.21, No.1, Winter/Spring 1997, p.63; *The Economist*, "Kuwait: They Voted," Vol.341, No.7987, October 12, 1996, p.50; Peter Kemp, "Education: Fears for the Future," *Middle East Economic Digest*, Vol.41, No.13, March 29, 1997, p.5.

[127] For a recent and detailed discussion of economic policies in the six Gulf states see Cyrus Sassanpour, Policy Challenges in the Gulf Cooperation Council Countries, Washington DC: International Monetary Fund, 1996; Nigel Andrew Chalk, Mohamed A. El-Erian, Susan J. Fennell, Alexei P. Kireyev, and John F. Wilson, Kuwait: From Reconstruction to Accumulation for Future Generations, Washington DC: International Monetary Fund, 1997; Hossein Askari, Maha Bazzari, and William Tyler, "Policies and Economic Potential in the Countries of the Gulf Cooperation Council," pp.225-255 in Nemat Shafik, (ed.), *Economic Challenges Facing Middle Eastern and North African Countries*, London: Macmillan Press LTD, 1998.

An increasing realization of the need to diversify resources by introducing industrialization and financial and commercial services, as well as the growing conviction that the private sector plays a crucial role in securing improved economic performance, has reinforced the need to nationalize the labor force. For the last several years, there has been talk of the "Bahrainization," "Saudization," and "Omanization" of the labor force. The general goal of these policies is to make it more expensive and harder for private corporations to hire foreigners and simultaneously to raise the technical skills and qualifications of the indigenous labor force.

To consolidate this policy of greater dependence on national manpower, requires at least three steps. First, a slow process of changing public attitude toward vocational education must be pursued. Recently, both King Fahd of Saudi Arabia and Sultan Qaboos of Oman called on their citizens to be more willing to appreciate manual work. Second, a balance between technical training and "academic" learning needs to be achieved. More funds should be invested in professional and scientific education. Gulf monarchies need fewer Ph.D.s and more mechanics. Third, women should be integrated into the labor force. The high ratio of educated women should be reflected in the labor and in public life in general.

THE GENDER GAP

A fundamental social change in the contemporary Persian Gulf is the emergence of women in the previously exclusively male world of public affairs. Education is an important and visible component of this change.[128] In considering women's education and their changing social role, three main questions emerge. How successful have women been in gaining their share of public education? Who is behind this momentum and what is the impact of more educated women on the political systems?

Given the varying degrees of conservatism among the six Gulf societies, no one uniform policy has been implemented in regard to women's education. In countries such as Bahrain and Kuwait, women gained the right to be

---

[128] Ralph H. Magnus, "Societies and Social Change in the Persian Gulf," p.406, in Alvin J. Cottrell, (ed.), *The Persian Gulf States*, Baltimore: The Johns Hopkins University Press, 1980.

educated at an earlier date and with little opposition. By contrast, in the more conservative Saudi Arabia, granting the right of public education to women took longer and caused serious debate. Objections from concerned parents and ulama (religious scholars) to girls' schools, based on the fear that they might have undesirable effects on girls, delayed the establishment of these schools by the government until 1960. In order to open girls' schools, force was used against some conservative elements and the ulama were given the right to administer the schools.[129] Two years later, in 1962, four women were allowed to join a Saudi institution, King Saud University.[130] Since then, Gulf women have made dramatic advances as can be seen by their relatively high level of literacy (table I) and by the number of female students enrolled at all levels of education.

This impressive achievement does not mean that the conservatives have lost their influence over women's education. They have not. Still today, the purpose of educating girls in some of the Gulf monarchies is to bring them up in a proper Islamic way, to perform their duties in life: as ideal and successful housewives and good mothers, prepared to do things which suit their nature, like teaching, nursing and giving medical treatment.[131] Accordingly, at the university level women are allowed to specialize in education, liberal arts and medicine, but they are not offered specializations in fields such as engineering or geology because these graduates would be required to work with men or carry out duties in public. This strict policy against gender integration is also demonstrated by two other practices. Male teachers communicate with women students only through closed-circuit television. Second, women going abroad to study have to follow the mahram rule, whereby women are not allowed to travel without their closest male relative as a chaperon.

Despite these restrictions, women have made significant gains in public education. These achievements were largely made possible by initiatives taken by female members of the royal families, such as King Faisal's wife Iffat in Saudi Arabia, President Zayid's wife Fatima in the UAE, Emir Hamad's wife

---

[129] Torsten Husen, (ed.), *The International Encyclopedia of Education*, New York: Pergamon, 1994, p.406.

[130] Louay Bahry, "The New Saudi Woman: Modernizing in an Islamic Framework," *Middle East Journal*, Vol.36, No.4, Fall 1982, p.512.

[131] Eleanor A. Doumato, "Gender, Monarchy, and National Identity in Saudi Arabia," *British Journal of Middle Eastern Studies*, Vol.19, No.1, 1992, p.35.

Moza in Qatar, and Crown Prince Saad's wife Latifa in Kuwait. Without this royal encouragement, women in the Gulf would probably not have come as far and as fast as they have.

The spread of women's education has spurred their increasing integration into the labor force.

Table III
Women's Share of Labor Force (1970-1990)

Country	1970	1990
Bahrain	05	17
Kuwait	08	23
Oman	06	12
Qatar	04	11
Saudi Arabia	05	10
UAE	04	12
Developing Countries	37	39

Source: United Nations Development Program, *Human Development Report* 1997, New York: Oxford University Press, 1997, p.182.

Two conclusions can be drawn from the table. First, women in all six Gulf monarchies have made significant progress, doubling their share of the labor force in just two decades. Second, a comparison with other developing countries suggests that woman in the Gulf still have a long way to go. It is also worth mentioning that the rising number of educated and working women has had a positive spillover on women's political rights. At the time of this writing, Iran (1963) and Iraq (1967) are the only Gulf states in which women can vote. In the six monarchies, important steps have been taken toward achieving women's suffrage. Not surprisingly, Kuwait, the only state with an elected legislature, has taken the lead. In 1982 a bill was presented to the National Assembly requesting an amendment of the Electoral Law to allow women to vote. The bill was rejected 27 to 7 with 16 abstentions.[132] In 1997 a similar bill was introduced. This time, a strong argument for enfranchisement has been made based on the important role Kuwaiti women played in resisting the Iraqi

---

[132] Haya Al Mughni, Women in Kuwait: *The Politics of Gender*, London: Saqi Books, 1993, p.132.

occupation. Consequently, the argument goes, those who were willing to give their lives for their country should have the right to a say in its political future.[133]

In Oman, two women, Shukur bint Muhammad Al Ghamari and Tayba bint Muhammad Al Ma'wali were nominated in 1994 as members of the Omani Consultative Council by Sultan Qaboos.[134] In Bahrain, Munira Al Fakhro, a professor at the University of Bahrain with a Ph.D. from Columbia University, and other prominent figures, have been active in mobilizing public opinion and urging the government to restore an elected assembly in which women can vote and hold elected office.[135] In the United Arab Emirates, women have been allowed to join military academies to train in various paramilitary functions.[136] Finally, in conservative Saudi Arabia, in contrast to a general stereotype, women have made significant progress, particularly in business and the professions. In 1995, it was estimated that 40 percent of the kingdom's private wealth was owned by women.[137] The number of women registered with the Riyadh Chamber of Commerce has increased more than five times in the last few years.[138] Despite the fact that women in the Gulf have not achieved full political rights, the substantial rise in their educational level has increased their participation in public life, which has been incrementally transformed into political leverage.

---

[133] Faris Glubb, "Kuwait: Towards Votes for Women," *Middle East International*, No.543, February 7, 1997, p.15.

[134] Abdullah Juma Al Haj, "The Politics of Participation in the Gulf Cooperation Council States: The Omani Consultative Council," *Middle East Journal*, Vol.50, No.4, Fall 1996, p.268.

[135] Louay Bahry, "The Opposition in Bahrain: A Bellwether for the Gulf?" *Middle East Policy*, Vol.5, No.2, May 1997, p.47.

[136] Saleh Al Mani, "Of Security and Threat: Saudi Arabia's Perception," *Journal of South Asian and Middle Eastern Studies*, Vol.20, No.1, Fall 1996, p.87.

[137] *The Economist*, "Saudi Arabia: Silent Revolution," Vol.334, No.7900, February 4, 1995, p.39.

[138] Ibid.

PROSPECTS FOR THE FUTURE

Both the discussion and figures presented in this study illustrate the presence of two contradictory characteristics in the social fabric of the modern Gulf societies. All six monarchies have succeeded in dramatically increasing literacy rates in a short period of time. Furthermore, the high level of student enrollment at all levels is impressive. Measured by the quantity of education, the six Gulf states have made great strides. But this is not the whole story. There are some basic holes in this educational fabric. The discord between religious and secular schooling, between academic learning and the job market, and between women's education and their role in public life are important sources of tension in all six Gulf societies.

In the near future, this tension is likely to become more intense for two reasons. First, the high population growth rate in all six states means there will be more graduates and more job seekers. The current economic policies and systems have failed to generate enough jobs to keep up with the growing number of young people. Second, the growing need to diversify and privatize the economic structure requires a more skilled and professional labor force. Bluntly, the current educational systems do not enable the indigenous populations to meet these needs. The socioeconomic and political tensions produced by the current discordance could threaten the stability of the ruling regimes. The six Gulf monarchies need to reform their educational systems to achieve coherence between their educational goals and their socioeconomic needs.

Chapter 5

THE GULF MONARCHIES:
THE SUCCESSION QUESTION

The Gulf region is simultaneously very important and especially volatile. Most other places in the world are one or the other. Because of this combination, the region has occupied a central stage in world policy for the last several decades. The fluctuation of oil prices, the attempts to introduce economic adjustment programs and to reduce dependence on oil, the petitions by different opposition groups, and the diversity of defense strategies and arms stockpiling have all been the focus of a growing body of literature and policy-makers from all over the world.[139]. However, surprisingly very few studies have focused solely on the question of succession. Given the general absence of independent political institutions such as political parties in all the six Gulf monarchies (Bahrain, Kuwait, Oman, Qatar, Saudi Arabia, and the United Arab Emirates,) the royal families have enjoyed tremendous power. Accordingly, any analysis of the Arab Gulf states' domestic and foreign policies should include the leadership as an important variable, if not the most important one. The change in policy is less likely to come from opposition groups, technocrats, or the army. Rather, a change, if it happens, is more likely to be initiated from within the royal families themselves. Louis XIV's dictum, "Le 'etat c'est moi" applies strongly to the six monarchies.

---

[139]For example see M. E. Ahrari, Change and Continuity in the Middle East, London: Macmillan Press LTD, 1996; M. Jane Davis, (ed.), *Politics and International Relations in the Middle East*, Aldershot, UK: Edward Elgar, 1995; and F. Gregory Gause, *Oil Monarchies: Domestic and Security Challenges in the Arab Gulf States*, New York: Council on Foreign Relations Press, 1994.

In addition to the central role the royal families play in their political systems, the question of succession will confront the Gulf regimes, and the rest of the world, over the next few years given the fact that the majority of the current and potential leaders are in their late sixties and seventies. Equally important is the lack of an institutionalized mechanism for change. In most cases the process of transferring power from one ruler to another has been done in an arbitrary fashion. However, In 1992 and 1996 Saudi Arabia and Oman respectively, issued new rules to regulate the change in leadership but it is still too early to make any assessment.

Therefore, this chapter focuses on the royal families in the six Gulf monarchies as the main unit of analysis. The objective is to examine how they have been able to stay in charge of their societies for hundreds of years and if they are facing a "succession crisis" in the near future. Two caveats should be taken into consideration from the outset. First, the individual rulers (king, emir, sultan) are not the sole decision-makers. Instead different members in the royal families participate in the process of policy-making and policy-implementation. Therefore, throughout this study the monarchies will be treated more as institutions and less as individual rulers. Second, there is severe lack of data on the economic and political orientations of the Gulf rulers and the internal dynamics within the royal families. The balance of power within each dynasty is unknown and is left to academic and journalistic speculation. There is no official documentation of any family quarrel. The health of the head of states is considered a matter of top national security and, again, is left for public speculation.

SUCCESSION QUESTION: AN OVERVIEW

In the closing years of the twentieth century, none of the six Gulf dynasties seems to be in a real danger of losing power to any contender. Admittedly, there are opposition movements in all of them and dissatisfied individuals and groups. Still any talk about overthrowing a royal family should be seen as an exaggeration. The opposition is too divided and too weak to pose a credible threat to the political establishment. On the other side, the ruling regimes enjoy tremendous financial and political resources. However, this relative lack of a credible threat to the Gulf regimes should not be taken for granted. Another important source of danger is the intra-family quarrels. A brief review of the transition of power from one ruler to another in each of the Gulf monarchy should highlight the magnitude of this challenge.

BAHRAIN

The political environment in Bahrain reflects a number of historical and geo-political characteristics which together explain the role the royal family plays in the political system and the, relatively speaking, high level of political violence in comparison with the other Gulf monarchies. First, unlike the other states, the majority of the population in the archipelago are Shia'a who are governed by a Sunni royal family.[140] Naturally, there are claims of sectarian discrimination. Second, this royal family, Al khalifa, did not come to power from within the society, rather, it came as a result of conquest when Ahmad Ibn Khalifa, the founder of the dynasty, invaded Bahrain in 1783.[141] This has contributed to the absence of strong bonds or traditional dialogue between the royal family and the people. Third, oil was discovered in Bahrain in 1932, earlier than in the other Gulf monarchies. However, oil fields have almost been depleted and the prospects for substantial reserves are dim. These limited financial resources have had devastating impact on the political stability. On one side, they worsened the socio-economic conditions. On the other side, they restrained the royal family's ability to buy off the opposition. Given these characteristics; sectarian division, the establishment of the dynasty, and the limited oil revenues; the Al Khalifa royal family has tried to overcome any inter-family quarrel in order to confront these unfavorable conditions. Thus, since 1783, when Al Khalifa took power in Bahrain, there has been very little violence on the top. During these years, Manama has had eleven rulers, only one was killed and another was deposed. The others died naturally and power was transformed in a peaceful manner. Equally important, in the last several decades the law of primogeniture has been applied. Thus, the transition of

---

[140] The Shia'a represent %70 and the Sunni %30 of the population. Central Intelligence Agency, *The World Factbook*, Washington DC: US Government Printing Office, 1998, p.33.

[141] Rosemarie Said Zahlan, *The Making of the Modern Gulf States*, London: Unwin Hyman, 1989, p.82.

power from Emir Isa Ibn Sulman to his son Hamad is not subject to any speculation and is expected to be smooth.

KUWAIT

In the closing years of the millennium Kuwait is the only Gulf monarchy with an elected national assembly. Generally speaking, the emirate has always adopted a more liberal domestic and foreign policies than its more conservative neighbors. Several developments have played a role in shaping the Kuwaiti political system. First, more than the other Gulf states, Kuwait has always been exposed to external threat to its mere existence even before it became independent in 1961. Its location next to the three regional powers, Saudi Arabia, Iraq, and Iran, has made the country subject to military threats and attacks by these states as had been demonstrated early in the century (Saudi Arabia[142]), during Iran-Iraq War (Iran), and, more bluntly, by the Iraqi invasion in August 1990. This continuous real perception of an external threat has facilitated and re-inforced an internal unification of the Kuwaiti people behind the leadership of the Sabah dynasty. Second, to a great extent the history of the royal family is an integrated part of the state. Literally, the former created the latter. Put it differently, Kuwait was not inhabited until Sabah Ibn Jabir, the founder of the dynasty, moved there from central Arabia and established both the royal family and the state.[143] This overlap between them has enhanced the legitimacy of the rulers in Kuwait.

This legitimacy has been further consolidated by the overwhelming peaceful manner of passing the crown from one ruler to another. In its, almost, two centuries and a half history, the Al Sabah ruling family has experienced less violence than all the other Gulf dynasties. Since 1750, the country has had thirteen rulers, twelve of them died naturally and only one was killed in a "palace coup" in 1896. Furthermore, since 1915 some rules of succession have

---

[142] In 1922 at a conference held in Ujair (Hasa) two-thirds of the land claimed by Kuwait was given to Ibn Saud who later founded the modern state of Saudi Arabia. See Rosemarie Said Zahlan, "King Abd Al-Aziz's Changing Relationship with the Gulf States during the 1930s," pp.58-74, in Tim Niblock, (ed.), *State, Society and Economy in Saudi Arabia*, New York: St. Martin's Press, 1982.

[143] Ibid., p.80.

been established and applied. According to these traditions the rulers of Kuwait are selected from the descendants of Jabir (1915-1917) and Salim (1917-1921) and both succeeded their father Mubarak (1896-1915). In 1965 an exception occurred when Sabah Ibn Salim (1965-1977) succeeded his brother Abdullah (1950-1965). The current Emir is from the Jabir clan and the Heir Apparent is from the Salims. Thus, a family quarrel is not expected.

OMAN

The political system in Muscat is different in many aspects from its neighbors. Unlike the other Gulf monarchies, Oman has long traditions of central authority which go back hundreds of years ago. Furthermore, the majority of Omanis adhere to the Ibadhi sect.[144] For a long time in the Sultanate's history both the political and religious authorities were united which added to the absolute power the rulers have enjoyed.[145] Said Ibn Taimur's reign (1932-1970) is a good illustration of this autocratic rulership. He tried to impose full isolation on Oman to maintain the status quo and to protect it from what he perceived as the threat of modernization. This style of governing incited an armed rebellion in Dhufar led by the Popular Front for the Liberation of Oman. This insurgency lasted for ten years and finally was defeated by Qaboos who overthrew his father in a palace coup in 1970. It is important to point out that unlike the great majority of political opposition to the Gulf regimes, the rebellion in Dhufar was against the ruling family and aimed at establishing a republican form of government.

Since his rise to power, Qaboos has consolidated the traditional strong ties between the Sultanate and Britain. The latter still is a main trade-partner to the

---

[144] In 684 Abdullah Ibn Ibad broke away from the extremist movement known as "Kharadjite" and formed his own movement and named it after himself, Ibadiyya. The Ibadis have since adopted an accommodative attitude toward other Muslims. Since the late eighth century, Oman has become the spiritual center of the movement. See B. Lewis, V. Menage, C. Pellat, and J. Schache, *The Encyclopaedia of Islam*, London: Luzac and Co., 1971, p.648.

[145] Since the late nineteenth century the political and religious authorities have been separated.

former.[146] At the same time, Oman imports most of its armaments from Britain.[147] More important, Qaboos has initiated an ambitious socio-economic developmental plans. Accordingly, huge public funds had been invested in building hospitals and schools in order to improve the standard of living. Furthermore, in the 1990s, Oman is the only Gulf monarchy where women serve in the Consultative Council.[148] This development should not be exaggerated. The Sultan still holds tremendous power in his hands.[149] This raises an important question regarding the issue of succession. The fact that Qaboos has neither sons nor brothers opens the door for speculation. These speculations have been fueled by the continuous rejection of the Sultan to appoint a heir apparent.[150] In order to address this concern, a new Basic Law was issued in late 1996. According to Article six the responsibility of choosing a successor lies in the hands of the Family Council.[151] Given the fact that the transformation of power in the family's long history has not always been peaceful, It is uncertain how the process will work when the need arises.

---

[146] International Monetary Fund, *Direction of Trade Statistics Yearbook*, Washington DC: International Monetary Fund, 1997, p.339.

[147] For details see the International Institute for Strategic Studies, Military Balance, New York: Oxford University Press, various years. And Stockholm International Peace Research Institute, *SIPRI Yearbook*, New York: Oxford University Press, various years.

[148] For a discussion of the Omani Consultative Council see Abdullah Juma Al Haj, "The Politics of Participation in the Gulf Cooperation Council States: The Omani Consultative Council," *Middle East Journal*, Vol.50, No.4, Fall 1996, pp.559-571.

[149] Sultan's Qaboos's birthday is also Oman's national day which underlines the close association between the ruler and the state.

[150] In 1997 Sultan Qaboos said that he had written down two names in descending order and put them in sealed envelopes in two different regions. See Judith Miller, "Creating Modern Oman," *Foreign Affairs*, Vol.76, No.3, May/June 1997, p.17.

[151] The author obtained a copy of the Basic Law in Arabic from the Information Attaché, Embassy of the Sultanate of Oman, Washington DC.

QATAR

Qatar was the scene for the only transformation of power in the Gulf monarchies in fourteen years. In June 1995 Hamad Ibn Khalifa deposed his father who was vacationing in Switzerland. This abdication underlines the lack of regularity in the Doha's recent political history. Since Al Thani dynasty has been in charge in Qatar in 1868, seven rulers had succeeded each other. The first three died naturally and the last three were deposed by a cousin and two sons. This troubled legacy points to the dominance of factionalism in the royal family in the last several decades. Furthermore, there were some indications of possible use of force to settle down the last transition of power. The deposed Emir, Khalifa, did not accept his overthrown from power and took some steps in order to get back his throne. These included transferring a huge sum of money (estimated between $3 to $7 billion) from the state's account to his own personal account.[152] In addition, in an attempt to gain support to his return, Khalifa visited the other five Gulf monarchies, Egypt, and Syria where he was given a royal reception. Finally, there were allegations (made by the current Emir) that Khalifa was assembling some military forces to reinstate himself.[153] An end to this uncertainty came with the announcement of a deal in October 1996 by which Khalifa is to be allowed to return to Qatar, along with his advisors, with an honorific title. In return, he will hand over most of his cash back to the state.[154]

The return of this fortune to the public treasury is of great significance. Recently, Qatar has embarked on ambitious scheme to develop its economic infrastructure. Unlike some other Gulf states, such as Bahrain, the future for Qatar looks very promising. With very small population, the country has the world's third-largest proven gas reserves after Russia and Iran.[155] These shining economic prospects can facilitate the process of economic and political reform which the new Emir has announced. Since he came to power

---

[152] *Financial Times*, "Qatar Sheikh Sees Cash As His Ace," January 11, 1996, p.5.

[153] *The Economist*, "The Gulf: Turbulent Waves," Vol.338, No.7954, February 24, 1996, p.45.

[154] *Middle East International*, "The Gulf: Reforms in Qatar and Oman," November 22, 1996, No.538, p.14.

[155] British Petroleum Company, *BP Statistical Review of World Energy*, London: British Petroleum Company, 1998, p.20.

in June 1995, the youngest ruler in the Gulf, Emir Hamad, has taken a number
of controversial initiatives in both domestic and foreign policies. In his first
decree after assuming power, Hamad approved the establishment of a formal
stock exchange, to be known as the Doha Securities Market. It was followed
by another decree providing for the creation of a new investment company in
which foreigners will be allowed to participate.[156] In a similar fashion,
elections for municipal councils will be held and will be considered for the
Consultative Assembly in the near future. In foreign policy, the new Emir has
adopted an independent line from that of Saudi Arabia. Qatar enjoys balanced
relations with both Iran and Iraq. The conflict with Bahrain over the Hawar
islands has not been resolved. Finally, in addition to Oman, Qatar has taken a
more reconciliatory attitude with regard to Israel than the other four Gulf
monarchies.[157]

SAUDI ARABIA

Saudi Arabia is the largest and most populous Gulf monarchy. In addition,
the kingdom enjoys tremendous economic leverage, given its immense oil
reserves and production. Accordingly, Riyadh has played a leading role on the
regional and international scene in the last several decades. Not surprisingly,
the question of succession in the kingdom has been a major concern to many
countries all over the world. Put it differently, the stability of the Gulf region
which is the main guarantee for the non-interruption of oil supplies is strongly
influenced by how the Saudi royal family handles the transition of power from
one ruler to another. Given the internal dynamics of the House of Saud and the
health conditions of its leaders, the succession question has become a subject
to a great deal of speculation and uncertainty. In order to examine the process
of transforming power in the kingdom three questions will be addressed. First,
what does the recent history of the royal family can tell us about this process?

---

[156] *Middle East Economic Digest*, "Qatar's New Emir Hastens Change," Vol.39,
No.29, July 21, 1995, p.2.

[157] This attitude by the Emir of Qatar which can be characterized as less hostile than
most of the other Arab states has been restrained since Binyamin Netanyahu
became Prime Minister in Israel in 1996.

Second, Does Riyadh face a succession "crisis?" Third, what direction will the dynasty take in the foreseeable future?

The modern-day Saudi Arabia was established by Abd Al Aziz Ibn Saud (1901-1953). The kingdom was created by an alliance between the Saudi royal family and the Ikhwan (brothers), the followers of Muhammad Ibn Abd Al Wahhab the founder of the Wahhabi movement.[158] Since then, this alliance between the political and religious authorities has played a significant role in maintaining and consolidating the legitimacy of both the state and the royal family. However, the political establishment confronted two challenges in transforming power from one king to another. The first one was in the early 1960s when King Saud was forced to abdicate to his brother King Faisal and the second one when the latter was assassinated by his nephew in 1975.

Upon his death in 1953, King Abd Al Aziz was succeeded by his son King Saud who did not have the charisma his father had. Furthermore, his lavish expenses from the country's oil revenues which he considered as his own personal income had almost bankrupted the treasury.[159] This financial disarray had important political implications and incited the royal family to take decisive steps in order to reassert its control. In the late 1950s two different visions on the future of the kingdom arose within the royal family. On one side, Prince Talal advocated the creation of a liberal parliamentary regime. On the other side, the then Crown Prince Faisal proposed an extensive socio-economic development within the framework of an authoritarian political system. The reinstatement of Faisal as Prime Minister in 1962 marked the victory of the latter approach.[160] Finally, on the request of sixty

---

[158] This name was given to the community by its opponents in the founder's lifetime and is used by western scholars. It is not used by its members in Arabia who call themselves Muwahhidun "unitarians." They regard themselves as Sunnis following the school of Ibn Hanbal, as interpreted by Ibn Taimiya, who attacked the cult of saints in many of his writings.

[159] Burke's Royal Families of the World, London: *Burke's Peerage* LTD, 1980, p.200.

[160] Tim Niblock, "Social Structure and the Development of the Saudi Arabian Political System," p.78 in Tim Niblock (ed.), State, Society and Economy in Saudi Arabia, New York: ST. Martin's Press, 1982.

princes and after a ruling by the ulama (religious scholars), Saud was obliged to abdicate in March 1964.[161]

The second important challenge to the Saudi royal family came in 1975 when King Faisal was assassinated, unexpectedly, by his nephew Prince Faisal Ibn Musa'id. Immediately, King Khalid replaced his brother and the killer, whose motives have never been disclosed, was beheaded. Khalid delegated most of his power to the Crown Prince Fahd who became King in 1982 after the former's death.

Two important conclusions can be drawn from these episodes (King Saud's abdication and King Faisal's assassination). First, like any big family, the Saudi dynasty is not united and differences and disagreements do exist. Second, the family has proven its ability to overcome these quarrels by acting in a collective manner and in collaboration with the religious establishment. This success raises the question of the royal family's capability to maintain its cohesive approach to face the potential challenge of transforming power from King Fahd to the next ruler. This issue gained attention in the mid 1990s when King Fahd was believed to suffer a stroke and, temporarily, delegated power to Crown Prince Abdullah.

Increasingly, Abdullah, the King's half-brother, has assumed the day-to-day operations of the government. This growing role of the Crown Prince raises speculations on his powerbase, policy, and relations with other members in the royal family. As the head of the National Guard for a long time, Abdullah has consolidated his ties with the tribe-chiefs. This close association with important base of power will enhance Abdullah's stand if/when he becomes a king. This should give him an additional leverage in any contention with the ulama and in conducting foreign policy as well. In his long political career, the Crown Prince has been identified more with Arab nationalism and less with Western powers. However, the strong relations between the kingdom and the West, particularly United States, are not expected to suffer any setbacks. Riyadh depends on Washington for its national security as has been demonstrated during and in the aftermath of the Gulf War. Thus, if there will be change in Saudi policy after King Fahd, it is likely to be more in style and less in substance. In other words, Abdullah is

---

[161] James Buchan, "Secular and Religious Opposition in Saudi Arabia," p.114 in Tim Niblock (ed.), *State, Society and Economy in Saudi Arabia*, New York: St. Martin's Press, 1982.

not expected to introduce any fundamental changes in the kingdom's policy. Finally, a power-struggle between Abdullah and the so-called "Sudairi seven" is not likely. These are the sons of Abd Al Aziz from his favorite wife Hussah Bint Al Sudairi: King Fahd, Prince Sultan, Prince Nayif, Prince Salman, Prince Ahmad, Prince Abd Al Rahman, and Prince Turki.[162] As far as it stands at the end of the twentieth century, the crown is expected to pass from Fahd to Abdullah to Sultan. However, the three men are over seventy years old and the real challenge to the royal family will come after their departure which is likely to be fast and in short intervals.

It does not help to speculate on when any leader might die, but one can expect that in the near future the throne will pass to the next generation of the royal family. The four kings who ruled the kingdom are all the sons of the founder Abd Al Aziz. The jockeying for power among their children, the grandchildren of Abd Al Aziz the founder of the kingdom, is already underway. This process has been complicated by the Basic Law of Government which King Fahd issued in March 1992. According to Article Five, "Rule passes to the sons of the founding king and to their children's children. The most upright among them is to receive allegiance.[163]" In addition, the Law states that, "The King chooses the heir apparent and relieves him of his duties by royal order.[164]" Thus, the new regulations assert the king's right to appoint and dismiss his successor. This process will be based on suitability instead of seniority. In closing it is important to point out that these rules will not be applied to Abdullah and Sultan since they have already been chosen. Rather they will be considered in selecting whoever would succeed them. This makes the future of succession in the kingdom uncertain.

---

[162] Andrew Rathmell, "Saudi Arabia Faces More Turbulent Times," *Jane's Intelligence Review*, Vol.8, No.4, April 1996, p.165.

[163] Simon Henderson, *After King Fahd: Succession In Saudi Arabia*, Washington DC: The Washington Institute For Near East Policy, 1994, p.55.

[164] Ibid., p.55.

UNITED ARAB EMIRATES

The United Arab Emirates is the only state in the region to adopt a federal system of government when Abu Dhabi, Dubai, Sharjah, Ajman, Umm Al Qaywayn, and Fujayrah formed a union following the British withdrawal from the region in December 1971. Ras Al Khaymah, the seventh member of the UAE, joined the federation in February 1972.[165] Since then, Abu Dhabi, the largest, wealthiest, and most populous member in the federation has taken a leading role in promoting economic, political, and military integration between the different emirates. Accordingly, its ruler, Zayid Ibn Sultan has been the President of the United Arab Emirates since 1971. In a few years, President Zayid has succeeded in transforming his country from a state of poverty to an incredible wealth. Two important developments contributed to this swift success. First, the commercial production of oil since the early 1960s provided the country with a substantial financial resources. This immense wealth remained idle under Shakhbut leadership (1928-1966), who sought to preserve the status quo by preventing any measure of modernization. This policy was opposed by the ruling family which decided to replace Shakhbut by his younger brother Zayid. Second, the end of violence among members of the royal family in Abu Dhabi. The dynasty has had thirteen leaders. Only three died naturally, the other twelve were either killed or deposed by relatives. The Shakhbut's long reign and the peaceful manner in which power was transformed to Zayid provided the country with much needed political stability at the top of the political system.[166] When President Zayid Leaves the scene his son and Heir Apparent Khalifah is expected to succeed him both as Emir of Abu Dhabi and President of the UAE without any challenge.

---

[165] *Europa Yearbook*, The Middle East And North Africa, London: Europa Publications Limited, 1996, p.1030.

[166] It is worth mentioning that President Zayid's mother made her sons swear not to kill each other in their fighting over political power. See Burke's Royal Families of the World, London: *Burke's Peerage* Limited, 1980, p.113.

CONCLUSION

The preceding survey examined the changes on the top in each of the six Gulf monarchies. The goal has been to highlight the pattern of passing the throne from one ruler to another in each state and to analyze any common characteristics between the six of them. A number of conclusions can be drawn from this discussion. First, the history of the Gulf states is, to a great extent, intertwined with that of the royal families. For example, Saudi Arabia was named after the founder of the dynasty and Kuwait was literally created by the Sabah family. This explains how some members in the ruling families perceive the state as a "family enterprise." Furthermore, some rulers, both in the past and at present, present themselves, and are seen by some of their citizens, not as the head of a complex military/bureaucratic apparatus but as the father or a chief of an extended family. With the passing of time and because of the growing impact of modernization the former perception should gain ground at the expense of the latter. Second, factionalism, jealousy, and rivalry are common characteristics of the six dynasties. Like any family, particularly the big ones, different members have conflicting visions and interests. What makes the competition more intense for the royal families is what is at stake. Princes vie with each other over the control of immense financial and political resources. The findings of this study confirm this fiery competition on the top of the political systems in the Gulf states. Since their creation, the Gulf monarchies had experienced fifty-eight transitions of power, thirty-three (%56.89) were conducted in a peaceful manner and the other twenty-five (%43.10) were carried out by palace coups. The level of violence varies from one dynasty to another but it does exist in all of them. The absence of rules of succession or law of primogeniture has contributed to this arbitrary fashion of transforming power. In many cases the strongest member in the family or a compromise candidate became the successor. Third, given the low level of institutionalization (i.e. lack of autonomous political institutions), the transition of power from one ruler to another has had a significant impact on the economic and political orientation of the state. Put it differently, succession does make a difference. Comparing the conservative approaches of Shakhbut (UAE), Said (Oman), and Saud (Saudi Arabia) with the vigorous attempts by their successors Zayid, Qaboos, and Faisal to modernize their societies substantiates this conclusion. Fourth, in four states (Bahrain, Kuwait, Saudi Arabia, and the UAE) the rulers are in their seventies and eighties. This suggests that probably within a decade they will be succeeded by a younger generation. This expected process of a generational change has promoted some observers to speculate on potential splits within the ruling families and attempts by some dissatisfied members to appeal and mobilize some segments in their societies for support.[167] This study takes different stand from this line of analysis. In their long history in power, the throne had passed from one generation to another and the differences were contained within the ruling families. In other words, an important contention of this study is that preserving the rulership of the royal families has always surpassed the interests of individual princes.[168] Finally, there is no credible threat to any of the six Gulf monarchies. There is rising discontent among different groups within the Gulf societies but it is neither intense enough nor organized enough to pose a real challenge to the political establishment. The royal families have proven their capability to wither many storms. In addition to internal splits, Gulf dynasties have survived the challenges from Nasser of Egypt, Khomeini of Iran, and Hussein of Iraq. Rather, the main dilemma facing them in the foreseeable future is how to sustain an authoritarian form of government in a rapidly modernizing society. Oil boom has accelerated the process of social mobilization. Gulf populations are better educated and well-exposed to international media. It is uncertain how long they can remain excluded from participation in their political systems. Only time can tell.

---

[167] Gregory Gause, "The Gulf Conundrum: Economic Change, Population Growth, and Political Stability in the GCC States," *Washington Quarterly*, Vol.20, No.1, Winter 1997, p.159.

[168] Other observers reach similar conclusions. See Michael Collins Dunn, "Is The Sky Falling? Saudi Arabia's Economic Problems And Political Stability," *Middle East Policy*, Vol.3, No.4, April 1995, p.36. And Tim Niblock, "Social Structure And The Development Of The Saudi Arabian Political System," p.101, in Tim Niblock, (ed.), *State, Society and Economy in Saudi Arabia*, New York: St. Martin's Press, 1982.

APPENDIX - SUCCESSION IN THE GULF MONARCHIES

BAHRAIN

Year	Ruler	Relation	Comment
1783-1796	Ahmad Ibn Khalifa		died
1796-1800	Sulman Ibn Ahmad	Son	died
1810-1825	Abdullah Ibn Ahmad	Brother	died
1825-1834	Khalifa Ibn Sulman	Nephew	died
1834-1867	Muhammad Ibn Khalifa	Son	died
1867-1869	Ali Ibn Khalifa	Brother	killed by a cousin
1869-1869	Muhammad Ibn Abdullah	Cousin	deposed by a nephew
1869-1932	Isa Ibn Ali	Nephew	died
1932-1942	Hamad Ibn Isa	Son	died
1942-1961	Sulman Ibn Hamad	Son	died
1961-1999	Isa Ibn Sulman	Son	died
1999-	Hamad Ibn Isa	Son	

*From 1800 to 1810 Bahrain was ruled by Wahhabi appointed governors.
*Column 3 is the relationship with the previous ruler.
* Current ruler Hamad Ibn Isa was born in 1950.

KUWAIT

Year	Ruler	Relation	Comment
1750-1762	Sabah Ibn Jabir		died
1762-1814	Abdullah Ibn Sabah	Son	died
1814-1859	Jabir Ibn Abdullah	Son	died
1859-1866	Sabah Ibn Jabir	Son	died
1866-1892	Abdullah Ibn Sabah	Son	died
1892-1896	Muhammad Ibn Sabah	Brother	Killed by a brother
1896-1915	Mubarak Ibn Sabah	Brother	died
1915-1917	Jabir Ibn Mubarak	Son	died
1917-1921	Salim Ibn Mubarak	Brother	died
1921-1950	Ahmad Ibn Jabir	Nephew	died
1950-1965	Abdullah Ibn Salim	Cousin	died
1965-1977	Sabah Ibn Salim	Brother	died
1977-	Jabir Ibn Ahmad	Cousin	

*Current ruler Jabir Ibn Ahmad was born in 1926.

OMAN

Year	Ruler	Relation	Comment
1744-1783	Ahmad Ibn Said		died
1783-1786	Said Ibn Ahmad	Son	deposed by his son
1786-1792	Hamad Ibn Ahmad	Son	died
1792-1804	Sultan Ibn Ahmad	Uncle	killed by pirates
1804-1806	Badr Ibn Saif	Nephew	killed by a cousin
1806-1821	Salim Ibn Sultan	Cousin	died
1821-1856	Said Ibn Sultan	Brother	died
1856-1866	Thuwaini Ibn Said	Son	killed by his son
1866-1868	Salim Ibn Thuwaini	Son	deposed by a nephew
1868-1871	Azzan Ibn Qais	Nephew	killed by a cousin
1871-1888	Turki Ibn Said	Cousin	died
1888-1913	Faisal Ibn Turki	Son	died
1913-1932	Taimur Ibn Faisal	Son	deposed by his son
1932-1970	Said Ibn Taimur	Son	deposed by his son
1970-	Qaboos Ibn Said	Son	

*The current ruler Qaboos Ibn Said was born in 1940.

QATAR

Year	Ruler	Relation	Comment
1868-1878	Muhammad Ibn Thani		died
1878-1913	Jasim Ibn Muhammad	Son	died
1913-1949	Abdullah Ibn Jasim	Son	died
1949-1960	Ali Ibn Abdullah	Son	deposed by his son
1960-1972	Ahmad Ibn Ali	Son	deposed by a cousin
1972-1995	Khalifa Ibn Hamad	Cousin	deposed by his son
1995-	Hamad Ibn Khalifa	Son	

*The current ruler Hamad Ibn Khalifa was born in 1950.

SAUDI ARABIA

Year	Ruler	Relation	Comment
1901-1953	Abd Al Aziz Ibn Saud		died
1953-1964	Saud Ibn Abd Al Aziz	Son	deposed by a brother
1964-1975	Faisal Ibn Abd Al Aziz	Brother	killed by a nephew
1975-1982	Khalid Ibn Abd Al Aziz	Brother	died
1982-	Fahd Ibn Abd Al Aziz	Brother	

*The current ruler Fahd Ibn Abd Al Aziz was born in 1921.

UNITED ARAB EMIRATES

Year	Ruler	Relation	Comment
1761-1793	Dhiyab Ibn Isa		killed by a kinsman
1793-1816	Shakhbut Ibn Dhiyab	Son	died
1816-1818	Muhammad Ibn Shakhbut	Son	deposed by a brother
1818-1833	Tahnun Ibn Shakhbut	Brother	killed by a brother
1833-1845	Khalifa Ibn Shakhbut	Brother	killed by a kinsman
1845-1855	Said Ibn Tahnun	Nephew	deposed by a cousin
1855-1909	Zayid Ibn Khalifa	Cousin	died
1909-1912	Tahnun Ibn Zayid	Son	died
1912-1922	Hamdan Ibn Zayid	Brother	killed by a brother
1922-1927	Sultan Ibn Zayid	Brother	killed by a brother
1927-1928	Saqr Ibn Zayid	Brother	killed by a nephew
1928-1966	Shakhbut Ibn Sultan	Nephew	deposed by a brother
1966-	Zayid Ibn Sultan	Brother	

*The current ruler Zayid Ibn Sultan was born in 1918.

Sources: *Burke's Royal Families of the World*, London: Burke's Peerage LTD, 1980; Richard F. Nyrop, *Area Handbook for the Persian Gulf States*, Washington DC: US Government Printing Office, 1977; and *Gulf Monarchies' embassies in Washington DC*.

Chapter 6

IRAQ: UNCERTAIN FUTURE

President Saddam Hussein's decision to invade Kuwait in August 1990 has fundamentally changed the dynamics of his relations with several countries. The international coalition, led by the United States, dealt a heavy blow, but not a fatal one, to the regime in Baghdad. At the end of the fighting President Bush decided not to pursue the Iraqi president. Instead, the implicit (and occasionally explicit) American policy has been to impose strict economic sanctions which would create intolerable conditions for the Iraqi people. This, it was expected, should incite the population to overthrow Saddam Hussein.

Several years under the sanctions, the Iraqi leader still is in power. Instead of collapsing, the Hussein's regime has consolidated its grips on power, resumed territorial sovereignty over most of the country and has expanded the scope of its foreign relations. Put differently, at the end of the 1990s the Iraqi regime is more stable than it was shortly after the Gulf War. Washington policy (mainly supported by London, Riyadh, and Kuwait) has failed to bring down the Iraqi leader or to impose any fundamental change in the characteristic of his regime. Equally important, the problem of stability in the Gulf region has been equated to the longevity of Hussein's regime. In other words, some analysts have asserted that there will not be stability as long as the Iraqi president is in power.

This study adopts a cautious approach toward this perception. There is no doubt that the Iraqi leader made a number of miscalculations which have had disastrous consequences to his country. According to a prominent scholar of the region, "this man alone is responsible for hundreds of thousands of deaths, untold suffering, and a setback to his country's economic prospects that will take decades to repair.[169]. It is ironic that in Iraq, the country with the second largest oil reserves in the world after Saudi Arabia, people have suffered from intolerable economic conditions for the last several years. The Iraqi leader bears the responsibility for much of this suffering.

At the same time, it is important neither to over-emphasize Saddam Hussein's role nor to underestimate the impact of other factors on Baghdad's policy. Before Saddam rose to power in the 1970s, Iraq was not a liberal democracy. At one point, he will leave the scene and will not be succeeded by an Iraqi Thomas Jefferson. Rather, another authoritarian leader is likely to take his place. In other words, before Saddam and after him important socioeconomic characteristics have continued to shape the Iraqi policy. In the following an attempt is made to analyze these characteristics and how they might influence the choices available for any future leadership in Baghdad. In this context, the evolution of the political system in Baghdad will be discussed. Second, the demographic composition of Iraq will be analyzed. Third, Baghdad's dependence on its neighbors to export oil will be examined. Finally, the border-disputes between Iraq and two of its neighbors (Iran and Kuwait) will be reviewed.

THE EVOLUTION OF THE POLITICAL SYSTEM IN BAGHDAD

For four centuries Iraq was part of the Ottoman Empire. In the aftermath of the First World War, Britain became the dominant power in Iraq for a transitional period. In 1921 a monarchy was proclaimed under the leadership of King Faisal Ibn Hussein. Officially Iraq became independent and joined the League of Nations in 1932 but the British influence continued to prevail until the violent overthrow of the Hashimite dynasty in 1958. The British legacy left two significant marks on the configuration of Iraq which explain the predominance of violence in the Iraqi domestic and foreign policies. First, the process of drawing the frontiers of the new state left it vulnerable to and dependent on the goodwill of its six neighbors. Since its creation back in the early 1920s, a consensus has not been reached on the final shape of the Iraqi state. As will be discussed shortly, over the years Baghdad has engaged in

---

[169]William Quandt, "The Middle East on the Brink: Prospects for Change in the 21st Century," *Middle East Journal*, Vol.50, No.1, Winter 1996, p.13."

border-disputes with its surrounding states. The second characteristic of the Iraqi body politic which came out of the British legacy is the absence of national coherence. The state is composed of several ethnic and religious groups. In a sense, the Iraqi domestic policy can be seen as an attempt to reach an agreement between these different groups on how they can live side by side and forge a national identity.

These two characteristics (lack of consensus on the configuration of the state and the presence of ethnic and religious cleavages) have contributed to a high level of instability in the Iraqi policy. The new regime, led by Abd Al Karim Qasim lasted for only five years. In 1963 Qassim was overthrown and assassinated by Abd Al Salam Arif who died in a helicopter crash in 1966. Abd Al Rahman Arif succeeded his brother but was overthrown and sent to exile in 1968 when the Baath Party orchestrated a coup d'etat led by Ahmad Hassan Al Bakr. After eleven years in office, Al Bakr was replaced by Saddam Hussein who has ruled Iraq since 1979. This irregular transition of power is illustrated in the following table

Table I
Accessions to Power in Iraq since 1921

Ruler	Reign	Comment
Faisal Ibn Hussein	1921-1933	died
Ghazi Ibn Faisal	1933-1939	killed in an accident
Faisal II Ibn Ghazi	1939-1958	assassinated
Abd Al Karim Qasim	1958-1963	assassinated
Abd Al Salam Arif	1963-1966	killed in an accident
Abd Al Rahman Arif	1966-1968	sent into exile
Ahmad Hassan Al Bakr	1968-1979	resigned
*Saddam Hussein	1979-	

* Saddam Hussein was considered the strong man in the political system since 1973.

The above table shows that Saddam Hussein has been in power longer than any of his predecessors. Indeed he has been at the helm in Baghdad longer than any other leader since Iraq became a nation-state in 1921.[170]

---

[170] Since Iraq was part of the Ottoman Empire since the sixteenth century and was ruled by different Islamic dynasties before that, it can be argued that Saddam

Ironically, in his long reign the country has experienced a state of "continuous crisis.[171]" Over the last two decades, Iraq went to war against Iran (1980-88), the international coalition (1990-91), and for most of the 1990s has been under heavy economic sanctions imposed by the United Nations (UN). This paradox raises the question of how Saddam Hussein has managed to politically survive all these years. In the Arab world context, where longevity is the rule not the exception, probably it is easier to explain why one leader is ousted from power than trying to speculate on why leaders stay in office as long as they do. Nevertheless, some factors might help understanding how, against all the odds, the Iraqi president still is in power.

These factors include favorite economic conditions in the 1970s, Saddam Hussein's style of rulership, the characteristics of the Iraqi opposition, and the reaction to the UN-sanctions. First, shortly after the Baath Party consolidated its hold on power in the early 1970s Iraq's revenues from selling oil skyrocketed from $513 million in 1970 to $7.6 billion in 1975 to $25 billion in 1980.[172] Given these immense financial resources, the Baath regime, like other oil producing states, embarked on ambitious social and economic development plans. The outcome had been a general improvement in the standard of living for the majority of the Iraqi people.[173] Second, Saddam Hussein has ruled through an unprecedented personalization of political power. The Iraqi president depends on a network of power based on kinship ties with Sunni Arabs, on long-standing friendships with Baathist fellow travelers, and most important of all, on his immediate family, the Takriti

---

Hussein has ruled Iraq, as national leader, longer than anybody else in its entire history.

[171] Adeed Dawisha, "Iraqi Politics: The Past and Present as Context for the Future," p.12, in John Calabrese, *The Future of Iraq*, Washington DC: The Middle East Institute, 1997.

[172] The figures for 1970 and 1975 are cited in Keith McLachlan, "Oil in the Persian Gulf Area," pp.218 & 220, in Alvin J. Cottrell, *The Persian Gulf States: A General Survey*, Baltimore: Johns Hopkins University Press, 1980. The figure for 1980 is from the Central Intelligence Agency, Handbook of International Economic Statistics, Washington DC: US Government Printing Office, 1998, p.94.

[173] For a similar argument see Ian S. Lustick, "The Absence of Middle Eastern Great Powers: Political 'Backwardness' in Historical Perspective," *International Organization*, Vol.51, No.4, Fall 1997, pp.653-683.

clan.[174] Third, partly because of Saddam's severe brutality the opposition to his rule has been weak and fragmented. Over the years Several opposition groups have vowed to overthrow the current regime. Instead, they have been fighting with each other and have proved ineffective. These include the Iraqi National Congress[175] (supported by the United States), the Iraqi National Accord (supported by the United States and Jordan), and the Supreme Assembly for the Islamic Revolution in Iraq (supported by Iran). The fact that most of these groups operate from outside Iraq and are sponsored by foreign powers has contributed to their weakness and lack of coherence. They have one goal in common, the ouster of Saddam Hussein, but their visions for the country after that vary widely. Finally, since the invasion of Kuwait in August 1990 sanctions were imposed on Iraq with an implicit goal to demonstrate to the Iraqi people that the reason for their misery is their leadership and the way to lift these sanctions is to overthrow Saddam Hussein. Although it is hard to provide any accurate assessment of how the Iraqi people respond to this implicit goal, the reports coming out of Baghdad suggest two trends. On one side, many Iraqis are absorbed by the daily struggle to survive the embargo. They have neither the energy nor the desire to participate in policy.[176] on the other side, some Iraqis blame the United States, not Saddam Hussein, for their misery. As one scholar states, "There is undoubtedly a 'Versailles complex' among Iraqis today which consists of a widespread and deep rooted perception that the country has been unjustly treated.[177]"

These reasons, among others, have contributed to the long reign of President Saddam Hussein. Equally important, it is uncertain how strong other players in the region really want the Iraqi leader out of power. It is true that Saddam Hussein is perceived as a threat to the stability of the region by several leaders. But, it is a threat that is being closely monitored by the

---

[174] Ahmed Hashim, "Iraq: Fin de Regime?" *Current History*, No.597, January 1996, p.14.

[175] For a thorough study of the Iraqi National Congress see Michael Gunter, "The Iraqi National Congress (INC) and the Future of the Iraqi Opposition," *Journal of South Asian and Middle Eastern Studies*, Vol.19, No.3, Spring 1996, pp.1-20. Also, for more information see the group's website: WWW.INC.ORG.UK/.

[176] For similar conclusion see Eric Rouleau, "America's Unyielding Policy toward Iraq," *Foreign Affairs*, Vol.74, No.1, January-February 1995, p.68.

[177] Volker Perthes, *Iraq Under Sanctions: A Regime Defiant, Briefing Paper*, No.40, London: The Royal Institute of International Affairs, February 1998, p.8.

international community.[178] Meanwhile, there is no guarantee that Saddam's replacement, when this happens, will act in different way. In addition to the leader's perception and style of governing, demographic and geo-political factors shape the Iraqi policy.

THE DEMOGRAPHIC COMPOSITION

The Iraqi population is composed of different ethnic groups (Arab 75%-80%, Kurdish 15%-20%, Turkoman, Assyrian and others 5%.[179]) The Kurds are the largest ethnic group in the Middle East without an independent state to represent them. A historical opportunity to establish a Kurdish state was sanctioned in the Treaty of Sevres in 1920. However, this part of the treaty was never implemented. Rather, under completely different circumstances a Kurdish state was created in 1945 but lasted for only few months. Nevertheless, Kurdish aspirations were not diminished. The Kurds have continued to pursue both diplomatic and violent methods to achieve their goal of independence and self-rule. Their struggle has particularly intensified since the late 1950s. The rise to power of successive nationalist and Baathist governments in Baghdad did not favor Kurdish demands. Thus, for several decades the relations between the Kurds and the central authority in Baghdad can be described as a series of uprisings and fragile peace.

In 1970 after several rounds of fighting and negotiation, the Kurdish leaders reached an agreement with the Iraqi government under which they would have been allowed to speak their own language and participate in the government. Most important, the agreement recognized the bi-nationalist characteristic of the Iraqi state.[180] After four years of reluctance and delay, the agreement was never fully implemented and the fighting between the

---

[178] M.E. Ahrari and Brigid Starkey, "Polarity and Stability in the Post-Cold War Persian Gulf," *The Fletcher Forum of World Affairs*, Vol.21, No.1, Winter/Spring 1997, p.140.

[179] Central Intelligence Agency, *The World Factbook*, Washington DC: US Government Printing Office, 1998, p.224.

[180] Oman Sheikhmous, "The Kurdish Question: Conflict Resolution Strategies at the Regional Level," in Elise Boulding, (ed.), *Building Peace in the Middle East, Boulder*, CO: Lynne Rienner, 1994, p.153.

government and the Kurds resumed. The Algiers Agreement (signed by Saddam Hussein and the Shah of Iran in 1975) ended the latter's support for the Kurdish opposition in the former. Consequently, the Baath regime had less resistance in crushing its Kurdish opponents. A few years later, the war between Iraq and Iran started and provided a "window of opportunity" for the Kurds to achieve their goal. The two prominent parties: the Kurdish Democratic Party (KDP), founded in 1946 by Mullah Mustafa Barzani[181], and the Patriotic Union of Kurdistan (PUK), established by Jalal Talabani in 1975 joined forces and formed the Iraqi kurdistan Front to lead the way for a self-rule. In the closing months of the war when Iraq had the upper hand and the international community was, more or less, in favor of Baghdad, Saddam Hussein turned his military might against the Kurds in an unprecedented fashion of ruthless revenge. This included an evacuation program by which many Kurds were forced to move to a more controllable areas, others were sent to other parts of Iraq against their will. This campaign of terror reached its peak in the Kurdish town of Halabja in March 1988. It is widely believed that the government used chemical weapons and thousands of people lost their lives.[182]

The Gulf crisis of 1990-91 provided a combination of both opportunities and risks to the Kurdish struggle. Shortly after the war Kurdish guerrilla took over a number of cities and towns in the north including the rich oil fields in Kirkuk. After heavy fighting, government forces were able to defeat the rebels. Fearing a repeat of the 1988 attack, many Kurds crossed the borders into Turkey and Iran. This time the drama of the Kurdish refugees was captured by the international media and incited world leaders to take some action in order to protect the Kurds. Based on a proposal by the, then, British Prime Minister John Major, a 'safe haven' was created. Iraq was prevented from flying its aircraft north of the 36 parallel.

Taking advantage of this international protection, several political parties participated in a free election in May 1992. For a while, the emerging democratic experiment in Kurdistan seemed promising. However, these expectations proved to be wrong and overly optimistic. Since 1994 the two

---

[181] Mullah Mustafa Barzani died in Washington in 1979 and was succeeded by his son Masoud.

[182] *Middle East Watch, Human Rights in Iraq*, New York: Human Rights Watch, 1990, p.144.

major Kurdish political parties the KDP and the PUK have been engaged in a dispute over turf and money. Frequently these disputes evolve into bloody confrontations. This led to a significant development in mid 1996. On August 31st, Barzani invited Iraqi forces to help him against his rival Talabani. Saddam Hussein did not hesitate to accept the invitation and to send his troops into the region. In the closing years of the century Northern Iraq is no longer a center for potential democratic opposition to Saddam Hussein. The Kurdish experiment with democracy has failed.

At least four reasons can explain this failure. First, the weak economic structure of the region. For many years Kurdistan received very little public investment. Purposefully, Baghdad had no interest in promoting economic prosperity in the Kurdish region. Even worse, the successive rounds of fighting between the government forces and the Kurdish rebels destroyed any economic infrastructure the region has ever had. This has deepened the Kurdistan's dependence on the outside, particularly on Turkey and Iran. In most of the 1990s, taxes on smuggled Iraqi oil to Turkey were the main source of income. Second, the division between the two major Kurdish political parties. The KDP and the PUK represent two distinctive constituencies in terms of geography (the Northwest vs. the Southeast) and in terms of religious affiliation (Naqshabandi vs. Qadiri.[183]) A genuine and long-term reconciliation between them is not likely any time soon.

Third reason for the continuous instability in the Kurdistan is the politics of regional powers particularly Syria, Turkey, and Iran. Each of these states has a huge Kurdish minority. Accordingly, a strong Kurdish basis in Northern Iraq would not be accepted by these regional powers because it might serve as a model for their own kurdish population. Furthermore, the frequent raids in the Northern Iraq by Iran (against the Kurdish Democratic Party of Iran 'KDPI') and by Turkey (against the Kurdish Workers' Party 'PKK') have further de-stabilized the region. Fourth, the policies and objectives of international powers, particularly the United States, are ambiguous. On one side Western leaders have obligated themselves to defend the Kurds from the ruthlessness of Saddam Hussein. On the other side, this commitment is

---

[183] Michael Collins Dunn, "The Kurdish Question: Is There An Answer? A Historical Overview," *Middle East Policy*: Vol.4, No.1&2, September 1995, p.75. And Michael M. Gunter, "The KDP-PUK Conflict In Northern Iraq," *The Middle East Journal*, Vol.50, No.2, Spring 1996, p.228.

restrained by the fear of antagonizing Turkey, a NATO member and an important ally for Western strategy in the Middle East and the Islamic World.

To sum up, the dilemma of assimilating the Kurds has confronted the central authorities in Baghdad for a long time. A common approach has been using coercive methods to force them to accept a national identity. No genuine attempt was made to accommodate the Kurdish demands. Under Saddam Hussein's leadership the violence against the Kurds reached an unprecedented level. The government's actions in Halabja and the rebellion of 1991 are good illustrations. Most important, the question of the Kurdish minority is still unanswered. No solution has been found. A forced assimilation can not guarantee long-term domestic stability. This issue is likely to haunt any future leadership in Baghdad until a satisfactory political solution, not a security one, is found. This unresolved domestic dilemma, with its regional implications, is aggravated further by strong dependence on neighboring countries in exporting oil.

OIL PIPELINES

At the end of the twentieth century, Iraq holds 112.5 thousand million barrels of oil (10.8 percent of world proven reserves,[184]) second only to Saudi Arabia. However, these immense resources cannot be fully utilized without access to the international market. This is exactly where the dilemma lies. Unlike the other Gulf states, Iraq is almost a landlocked country with a very small maritime outlet. Given this geopolitical vulnerability, Baghdad created an extensive system of oil shipment. Shortly after the creation of Iraq as a nation-state in the aftermath of the First World War, the British and French authorities, then in charge of most of the region, constructed pipelines linking Iraqi oil fields with terminals on the Mediterranean in Haifa, Tripoli, and

---

[184] British Petroleum Company, *BP Statistical Review of World Energy*, London: British Petroleum Company, 1998, p.4.

Banias (in Israel, Lebanon, and Syria respectively.[185]) Similarly, the subsequent Iraqi governments since the late 1970s have engaged in many projects to enlarge the country's safety network of pipelines. In 1977 a pipeline linking the northern oil fields in Kirkuk to the Turkish port Ceyhan on the Mediterranean came into operation, and in 1987 a parallel line was added. In addition to these lines to Turkey, Iraq constructed two pipelines which, skirting the territory of Kuwait, led to Saudi Arabia. The first was completed in 1985 and met the newly constructed Saudi "petroline" abutting Yanbu on the Red Sea. The second was built in 1990 paralleling the "petroline." Both were owned entirely by Iraq.[186] Finally, in 1995 Jordan and Iraq signed a tentative agreement to build a pipeline running from Iraq's Haditha pumping stations to Jordan's Zarqa refinery. In 1997, the two countries further agreed in principle to an expanded pipeline to supply a planned new refinery project in Jordan.[187]

These comprehensive and well-developed networks of pipelines show how dependent Baghdad is on the goodwill of its neighbors. Over the last few decades Iraq's strategic vulnerability has been demonstrated one time after another. The establishment of Israel in 1948 was an important reason for the closure of the Haifa line. The civil war in Lebanon and the antagonism between the two Baath regimes in Damascus and Baghdad were the main reasons for the closure of the Tripoli and Banias outlets. The Gulf War immobilized the pipelines across Turkey and Saudi Arabia and brought the shipping of the Iraqi oil to a halt. Furthermore, the war and the United Nations sanctions have severely limited the amount of oil Baghdad is allowed to produce as the following table shows.

---

[185] *The Economist Intelligence Unit, Country Profile: Iraq*, London: The Economist Intelligence Unit, 1996, p.23.

[186] George Lenczowski, "Major Pipelines in the Middle East: Problems and Prospects," *Middle East Policy*, Vol.3, No.4, April 1995, p.42.

[187] *Energy Information Administration, Country Report: Iraq*, Washington DC: US Government Printing Office, 1998, p.14.

Table II
Iraq Crude Oil Production (1970-1997)
(Thousand Barrels Per Day)

Year	Iraq	OPEC	%
1970	1,549	23,301	06.6
1971	1,694	25,209	06.7
1972	1,466	26,891	05.4
1973	2,018	30,629	06.5
1974	1,971	30,351	06.4
1975	2,262	26,771	08.4
1976	2,415	30,327	07.9
1977	2,348	30,893	07.6
1978	2,563	29,464	08.6
1979	3,477	30,581	11.3
1980	2,514	26,606	09.4
1981	1,000	22,481	04.4
1982	1,012	18,778	05.3
1983	1,005	17,497	05.7
1984	1,209	17,442	06.9
1985	1,433	16,181	08.8
1986	1,690	18,275	09.2
1987	2,079	18,571	11.2
1988	2,685	20,324	13.2
1989	2,897	22,071	13.1
1990	2,040	23,195	08.7
1991	0,305	23,275	01.3
1992	0,425	24,398	01.7
1993	0,512	25,119	02.0
1994	0,553	25,510	02.1
1995	0,560	26,092	02.1
1996	0,584	26,769	02.1
1997	1,187	28,362	04.1

Source: Energy Information Administration, *International Petroleum Statistics Report*, May 1998, table 4.1a, p.38.

The figures show how important Iraq is in the international oil market. Also, they demonstrate the immense reduction in production following the two wars (Iran-Iraq war and the Gulf war.) Since 1996 Iraq has been allowed to sell oil worth $2 billion every six months to satisfy the basic needs for its population (Resolution 986, known also as Food for Oil). In the early 1998 the United Nations Security Council approved a plan which increases the amount of oil the country can export to $5.2 billion. Given the level of destruction in the oil installations and the poor maintenance of the pipelines, it will take some time for the Iraqi government to achieve this level of production. Furthermore, in order to fully utilize its oil resources Baghdad needs to develop a "working relationship" with its neighbors. For the last several decades, these relations have mirrored regional tension over another interrelated issue: border disputes.

BORDER DISPUTES

For hundreds of years Baghdad, Basra, and Mosul (the largest Iraqi cities) were parts of the Ottoman Empire. In the early 1920s, they were united under the British mandate, which lasted until 1932 when Iraq became an independent state. Iraq shares a total of 3,631 km land boundaries with six countries (Iran, Saudi Arabia, Syria, Turkey, Kuwait, and Jordan) and has only 58 km of coastline.[188] This geopolitical configuration puts Baghdad in a disadvantaged state in comparison with its neighbors. Since the late 1930s, successive regimes in Baghdad have tried to overcome this geographical disadvantage. The result has been an almost uninterrupted state of hostility with its neighbors, particularly Iran and Kuwait.

A major source of conflict between Baghdad and Tehran has been the longstanding dispute over the Shatt al-Arab waterway, which runs into the Persian Gulf in the southern border area between the two countries. Whereas Iraq has traditionally claimed to have succeeded to the Ottoman Empire's jurisdiction over the whole waterway and that therefore the border between the two countries in this area runs along the eastern (i.e. Iranian) bank, Iran has consistently maintained that such a delimitation is not only unjust but also

---

[188] Central Intelligence Agency, p.204.

contrary to the Thalweg line principle (whereby riverine frontiers are defined as following the median line in the deepest channel.[189])

After several incidents in the early 1930s, the two countries tried to solve their dispute before the League of Nations. This attempt did not succeed, but the two sides negotiated and signed an agreement in 1937 which gave Iraq more control over the waterway.[190] Three decades later, in 1969, Iran abrogated the treaty. Given the military balance of power in the late 1960s between the two countries, Baghdad was not in a position to challenge Tehran. Furthermore, the strong support the Shah granted to the Kurdish rebels fighting the Iraqi government prompted the latter to accept the Iranian claims which were formalized in the Algiers Treaty of 1975.

At the end of the decade, the collapse of the Pahlavi regime and the establishment of the Islamic Republic resulted in a domestic turmoil. In an attempt to take advantage of this situation, Saddam Hussein abrogated the Algiers Treaty and started the eight-year war between the two countries. In 1988 the war ended with Iraq in full control of Shatt al-Arab. However, planning for the invasion of Kuwait and preparing for the war against the international alliance led by the United States, the Iraqi president made significant concessions to Iran and agreed to share sovereignty over the waterway. The Gulf War and its aftermath shifted the attention from the Iran-Iraq conflict over the Shatt al-Arab to the territorial dispute between Baghdad and Kuwait.

The border conflict between the two countries started several decades ago. A landmark agreement was reached in 1932 when Sheikh Ahmad al-Sabah, the ruler of Kuwait, and Nuri al-Said, the Iraqi Prime Minister, exchanged letters reaffirming the existing frontier between their two countries.[191] However, this agreement was not honored by the successive regimes in Baghdad. For example, in 1955 the Iraqi government sought to advance its

---

[189] John B. Allcock, Guy Arnold, Alan J. Day, D. S. Lewis, Lorimer Poultney, Roland Rance, D. J. Sagar, *Border and Territorial Disputes*, London: Longman, 1992, p.372.

[190] Richard N. Schofield, The Historical Problem of Iraqi Access to the Persian Gulf," in Clive H. Schofield and Richard N. Schofield, (eds.), *The Middle East and North Africa: World Boundaries*, London: Routledge, 1994, p.160.

[191] John Allcock, p.386.

frontier at the expense of Kuwait.[192] The opportunity came in 1961 when the latter became an independent state. The Iraqi Prime Minister General Qasim laid claim to all of Kuwait. A military confrontation almost took place but was averted when British and Arab forces were sent to protect Kuwait.

President Arif's rise to power in Baghdad in 1963 brought a relative ease of the tension between the two countries. The new leader confirmed his adherence to the 1932 agreement and to the sovereignty of Kuwait. Nevertheless, Baghdad renewed its claims over parts of Kuwait particularly the islands of Warba and Bubiyan on the Persian Gulf. Another military Iraqi attack against its southern neighbor was aborted in 1973 due to extensive Arab pressure. The Iran-Iraq war reinforced Baghdad's demands to acquire access to the islands of Warba and Bubiyan for military purposes. The two islands Would have given Iraq a great strategic advantage against its adversary Iran. Consequently, Tehran threatened to attack Kuwait if it agreed to cede or lease them. In response, no change occurred and the two islands remained under full Kuwaiti sovereignty.

In the aftermath of the Iran-Iraq war Baghdad intensified its claims over Kuwait and finally Saddam Hussein reached the wrong conclusion that the time was ripe to completely annex Kuwait. After the Gulf War, the United Nations created a commission to demarcate the boundaries between the two countries. Not surprisingly, the result of the UN commission's finding was to redraw the frontier in favor of Kuwait. Given the Iraqi defeat in the Gulf War and the pressure from Russia and France, the government in Baghdad recognized the sovereignty and frontiers of Kuwait in November 1994.

Three interrelated conclusions can be drawn from the preceding discussion, First, at the end of the twentieth century, the border disputes between Iraq and its neighbors should be seen as dormant not settled. The currently weakened and isolated Iraq has a limited power to challenge the status quo. But, one can speculate, if Baghdad were allowed to regain its military power and/or if the international community were unable or unwilling to maintain the sanctions, there is no doubt that Iraq would be likely to challenge what it perceives to be its geopolitical disadvantage, as it had done in the past. Second, since its independence in 1932, the Iraqi leaders have

---

[192] Richard Schofield, "The Kuwaiti Islands of Warba and Bubiyan, and Iraqi Access to the Gulf," p.166, in Richard Schofield, (ed.), *Territorial Foundations of the Gulf States*, London: University College London, 1994.

expressed dissatisfaction with the geographical configuration of their country. They have alleged that these frontiers were deliberately drawn by the British to ensure the weakness and vulnerability of Iraq, particularly in regard to access to the Gulf.[193] However, under Saddam Hussein's leadership, Iraq's border disputes with its neighbors were taken to the extreme. Baghdad quarreled with Tehran, Kuwait, and others for several decades over frontiers and other issues. But it was only in 1980 and 1990/91 (under Hussein's leadership) that these quarrels evolved into full-scale, devastating wars. Third, while a change in the leadership in Baghdad might ease the tension, it would be unlikely to solve the problem. Territorial stability will probably come to this part of the world only when Iraq reconciles itself to its disadvantageous position at the head of the Gulf, when it perceives itself as no longer 'squeezed out.[194]' It is uncertain when this might happen - if ever.

IRAQ AFTER SADDAM: CONCLUDING REMARKS

Since Iraq's invasion of Kuwait in August 1990 a lot has been said and written on the "re-structuring" of the political system in Baghdad. There has been a great deal of disagreement, but almost a universal consensus has been reached on two points which together represent a paradox for policy-makers. First, Saddam Hussein is untrustworthy and unpredictable. His long reign in Iraq has resulted in economic destruction and political instability both in Iraq and in the Persian Gulf region. Second, there is no valid option to replace him. All power contenders lack national popular appeal and are divided on ethnic, religious, and ideological lines. The possible triumph of some of them might endanger the territorial integrity of Iraq, which is seen as a sacred cow by the regional and international powers. These two paradoxical arguments have brought the process of restructuring the political system in Baghdad to a halt. Former American President George Bush said that he and others felt that a

---

[193] Charles Tripp, "The Future of Iraq and of Regional Security," p.149, in Geoffrey Kemp and Janice Gross Stein, (eds.), *Powder Keg in the Middle East*, Lanham, MD: Rowman and Littlefield, 1995.

[194] Richard N. Schofield, "Border Disputes In The Gulf: Past, Present, And Future," p.140, in Gary G. Sick and Lawrence G. Potter, *The Persian Gulf At The Millennium*, New York: St. Martin's Press, 1997.

sound military defeat would lead to the Iraqi leader's downfall and rightly admitted that he "underestimated the political staying power of President Saddam Hussein.[195]" Hardly anybody would have thought that the Iraqi leader would politically survive the defeat and remain in power several years after the war. Still, his political and physical survival can not be taken for granted. Other forces might have an opportunity to replace him. Given the volatility of the Iraqi political system, it is very risky to make any prediction. However, the interaction between the following factors is likely to shape the political environment in Baghdad in the early decades of the new millennium.

First, Saddam Hussein is a great survivor. Very few leaders in the world have ever been able to survive two wars. Saddam Hussein initiated both of them and the outcome had been disastrous in terms of human casualty and economic destruction. In the Gulf War he stood against almost the whole world and managed to outlive, politically, most of his rivals both inside and outside Iraq. At the same time, a collapse of the regime cannot be excluded particularly since it is so profoundly personalized. Saddam Hussein is not immune from a bullet of an assassin. Second, If President Saddam Hussein were removed there is the likelihood of a civil war. There is always a danger that Iraq might split as a nation. The disintegration of Iraq as a nation, with its geo-economic and geo-political significance is highly undesirable scenario. As one observer put it, "Iraq could become a Bosnia in the Middle East. A Bosnia with world-class oil potential.[196]" Almost eight decades of statehood have not succeeded in either overcoming the ethnic cleavages or confirming the territorial configuration of Iraq.

Third, another Sunni, Baathist, and military leader could gain power. Given the structure of the Iraqi political system and the dominant role and heavy control of the Sunnis, the Baathists, and the army on almost all sources of power within the country, it is likely that any alternative leadership to the present one will come from these constituencies. Saddam's successor will not institute a liberal democratic political system. Nevertheless, this potential regime, if it comes to power, will have at least two advantages. Like the

---

[195] New York Times, "Bush Says He Erred in Assuming Hussein Would Fall after War," January 15, 1996, p.A4.

[196] *Oil and Gas Journal*, "Editorial: The end game in Iraq," Vol.96, No.6, February 9, 1998, p.25.

current one, it will maintain the territorial integrity of Iraq, but unlike Saddam, the new leader will be more accepted by the regional and international powers.

Fourth, the current policy of severe economic sanctions is likely to be re-examined. Many members of the international coalition which fought Iraq in 1991 have been in favor of relaxation of the sanctions. In addition, the economic embargo, imposed on Iraq by the international community since its invasion of Kuwait in 1990, has not produced a kinder or gentler political system in Baghdad. The main characteristics of Hussein's regime have not changed. The policy needs re-assessment. Fifth, oil will play an important role in shaping the political future of Baghdad. In 1989, the last year before the invasion of Kuwait, Iraqi oil production stood at almost 3 million barrel per day (b/d). The complete lifting of the sanctions and Baghdad's resumption of its role in the international oil market would deal heavy blow to oil prices. Producing countries would suffer tremendously from such development. In the long-run, however, world demand is projected to grow at an average rate of 2 percent annually between 1995 and 2020 resulting in an increment of more than 45 million b/d.[197] The Iraqi oil will be crucial to meet this rising demand.

Regardless of who is in charge in Baghdad, Iraq is too important a country to be sidelined for such a long time. In the long-run the prosperity of the global economy and the security of the Persian Gulf region necessitate the rehabilitation and reintegration of Baghdad in the regional and international systems. There are tremendous obstacles, but it is worth the try.

---

[197] Energy Information Administration, *International Energy Outlook*, Washington DC: US Government Printing Office, 1998, p.4.

Chapter 7

IRAN AT THE TURN OF THE CENTURY: CONTINUITY AND CHANGE

Iran occupies a central position in the Persian Gulf. Over the past several decades, history, geography and natural resources have contributed to the rise of Tehran as a prominent regional power. With a population approaching 70 million people, the Islamic Republic is, by far, the most populous country in the Gulf. This has provided the country with a large pool of labor, a sizeable middle class, and equally important a big army. Furthermore, Iran has been blessed with tremendous natural resources. It holds 9 percent of world oil proven reserves and 15 percent of world natural gas proven reserves.[198]. Finally, Tehran is considered an important gate to energy-rich Central Asia region. Given all these facts, it can be argued that the stability of Iran has been crucial to many countries all over the world.

The Islamic revolution of 1979 represents a turning point in the long history of Iran. In a short period of time the clerical regime, founded by the late Ayatollah Khomeini, succeeded in establishing itself and in almost two decades was able to overcome or, more correctly, survive several internal and external challenges. More recently, May 1997, a presidential election was held and Muhammad Khatami won. His election has since incited a variety of expectations and speculations concerning the choices Iran might make under his leadership. Khatami, who will lead the Islamic Republic into the twenty-first century, has the opportunity to "re-shape" the country's domestic and foreign policy.

---

[198]British Petroleum, *BP Statistical Review of World Energy*, London: British Petroleum Company, 1998, pp.4 & 20.

In the following an attempt will be made to examine the evolution of the Islamic Republic sine 1979 and to address the question of whether Khatami has the will and the power to take Iran into a new direction. Two areas will be analyzed: the political structure and the economic reconstruction. The contention is that the clerical regime is experiencing a slow and gradual change toward what can be called 'political maturity.' This refers to the institutionalization of the political system, and the integration in the global economy. The trend is not firm and can be altered, but the opportunity does exist.

THE POLITICAL STRUCTURE

In the closing years of the 1990s, the clerical regime, founded by Ayatollah Khomeini almost two decades ago, seems well-established. The roots of this system go back to the 1979 revolution which overthrew the Pahlavi regime. A variety of socio-economic and political forces with diverse ideological orientations fought side-by-side against the Shah.[199] However, shortly after ascending to power the Islamic movement led by Khomeini succeeded in eliminating all the other forces and has since enjoyed almost full-control over the political system. Four interrelated characteristics of the clerical regime can be identified: A high level of continuity and institutionalization, lack of serious opposition, elite factionalism, and electoral illiberal democracy.

Continuity and institutionalization: Almost twenty years after the establishment of the Islamic Republic and nine years after the death of its founder the political system in Tehran can be seen as an embodiment of Khomeini's political and religious beliefs. Shortly after the collapse of the Pahlavi regime the Ayatollah created a number of institutions to strengthen and ensure the durability of the clerical system. Most of these institutions still are in place and continue to be run by Khomeini's students and followers. They include the faqih (Islamic jurisprudent), who is the spiritual guide of the nation, the president, the parliament (Majlis), Council of Experts, Council of

---

[199] For more details on these forces see Farhad Kazemi, "Models Of Iranian Politics, The Road To The Islamic Revolution, And The Challenge Of Civil Society," *World Politics*, Vol.47, No.4, July 1995, pp.555-574.

Guardians, Expediency Council, among others.[200] According to this system no single institution should be able to decide important political, economic, or ideological matters unilaterally.[201] Instead, there is some degree of check and balance between all of them. Still the ultimate power rests in the hands of the faqih.

Realizing the lack of a leader with his political and religious credentials, Khomeini gave his consent to amending the constitution shortly before his death in 1989. Accordingly, Khamenei became the Faqih and Rafsanjani resumed the presidency which has been strengthened with the abolishing of the position of prime minister. It is important to point out that this peaceful transfer of power in the aftermath of Khomeini's death to the dual leadership (Khamenei-Rafsanjani) and again in the presidential election of 1997 from the latter to Khatami suggests that the system works. In other words, the political institutions which were created in the early years of the revolution have contributed to a certain degree of domestic stability. This expanding control of the clerical regime has been enhanced by the absence of serious opposition to its rule.

Lack of credible opposition: Under the Pahlavi regime political opposition can be classified into three main categories: religious, liberal nationalist, and leftist. As has been mentioned above, all of them participated in the turmoil which led to the end of the Shah's reign. In the early years of the revolution, several bloody confrontations took place between these groups. Many prominent government leaders were killed in these clashes. In response, the clerical regime cracked down on all opposition groups. The Tudeh Party (Communist), for example, was banned in 1983. The collapse of the Soviet Union further contributed to the demise of the leftist opposition. Mujahidin-e Khalq (Holy Warriors of the People) were forced to flee Iran in 1982. They first went to Paris and then, in 1986, to Iraq, where they are currently based and from whose territory they attack Iran with the hope of undermining the clerical regime.[202] The Democratic Party of Iranian Kurdistan championed the demands for political and cultural autonomy. The clerical regime opposes

---

[200] Europa Publications, *The Middle East and North Africa*, London, 1997, p.490.

[201] Henner Furtig, "Iran-the Second Islamic Republic?" *Journal of South Asian and Middle Eastern Studies*, Vol.20, No.3, Spring 1997, p.23.

[202] Ahmad Ghoreishi and Dariush Zahedi, "Prospects For Regime Change In Iran," *Middle East Policy*, Vol.5, No.1, January 1997, p.90.

these demands on the ground that Islamic ideology calls for the unity not only of all Iranians but of all Muslims.[203] These opposing perceptions led to a bloody confrontation in the early 1980s.[204] Another important faction is the monarchists led by Prince Reza Pahlavi and residing mainly in California. This group enjoys some support from the Iranian expatriates but there is doubt on how many followers the monarchists have inside Iran.[205]

In contrast to these outlawed organizations, the Liberation Movement of Iran (Nehzat-Azadi) is tolerated by the regime. The group was founded in 1961 by Mehdi Bazargan, Iran's first post-revolution prime minister and currently is led by Ibrahim Yazdi.[206] It advocates liberal democracy and human rights within an Islamic framework. Other voices of opposition include Ayatollah Montazeri[207], Ayatollah Qomi[208] and the lay intellectual Abdol Karim Soroush.[209]

To sum up, several of the opposition groups operate from outside Iran (in the United States, Europe, and Iraq). This deprives them of direct contact with domestic constituencies and substantiates claims by the government that these groups serve the interests of foreign enemies to the Islamic regime. Moreover, they are disorganized and lack a strong leadership. Consequently, opposition

---

[203] Michael Collins Dunn, "The Kurdish 'Question': Is There An Answer? A Historical Overview," *Middle East Policy*, Vol.4, No.1, p.83, September 1995, p.83.

[204] Andrew Whitley, "Minorities and the Stateless in Persian Gulf Politics," *Survival*, Vol.35, No.4, Winter 1993, p.34.

[205] Ahmad Ghoreishi and Dariush Zahedi, p.92.

[206] Europa Publication, p.490.

[207] Ayatollah Montazeri was dismissed in 1989 as Khomeini's designated successor after criticizing some of the political practices (i.e., execution of political prisoners and suppression of the press). Since then he has been under virtual house arrest.

[208] Both Montazeri and Qomi (who was a revolutionary prosecutor in the early 1980s) wrote open letters in late 1997 criticizing Ayatollah Khamenei for his lack of religious credentials and poor policy management. See Saeed Barzin, "Theology and Football," *Middle East International*, No.564, December 5, 1997, p.15.

[209] For a detailed discussion of Soroush's criticism of the clerical regime see Robin Wright, "Iran's Greatest Political Challenge: Abdol Karim Soroush," World Policy Journal, Vol.24, No.2, Summer 1997, pp.67-74. Max Rodenbeck, "Is Islamism Losing Its Thunder?" *Washington Quarterly*, Vol.21, No.2, Spring 1998, pp.177-193. And Soroush's website on the Internet at www.seraj.com.

groups do not pose significant threat to the survival of the Islamic regime.[210] Equally important, is the fragmentation within the ruling political/religious establishment.

Elite Factionalism: Since the early days of the revolution the clerical regime has never been monolithic. Rather different factions have advocated a variety of approaches to deal with challenges facing Iran. However, given his charisma, Khomeini was able to contain the disagreements between these factions and to establish a degree of harmony between all of them within the political system. This delicate balance was disrupted with Khomeini's death. Three major factions can be identified: the conservatives who support economic liberalization but oppose close contact with the West particularly the United States, the radicals who stand for heavy government intervention in the economic system and strongly resist any dialogue with the West, and the technocrats who advocate economic reform, political liberalization, and social freedom.[211] The parliamentary elections in 1992 and 1996 and the presidential election in 1997 were contested by representatives of the three factions.[212] The outcome of all these elections confirms a two-fold political reality: First, after almost two decades in power the three factions are represented, more or less, in all political institutions. Second, the technocrats' share of power has been on the rise particularly at the expense of the radicals. Finally, this increasing intensity of power-jockeying suggests a growing level of pluralism within the ruling political/religious establishment in Tehran which raises the question of how democratic the clerical regime is

Electoral democracy vs. liberal democracy: Several political scientists have highlighted the differences between liberal democracy and electoral

---

[210] Fred Halliday, "An Elusive Normalization: Western Europe And The Iranian Revolution," *Middle East Journal*, Vol.48, No.2, Spring 1994, p.318.

[211] The policies of these factions have been examined in several sources. See for example Ahmed Hashim, *The Crisis of the Iranian State*, New York: Oxford University Press, 1995, pp.9-11.

[212] For an analysis of the 1992 elections see Farzin Sarabi, "The Post-Khomeini Era In Iran: The Elections of The Fourth Islamic Majlis," *Middle East Journal*, Vol.48, No.1, Winter 1994, pp.89-108. For 1996 elections see Kathy Evans, "Will the Mullahs Move On?" *The Middle East*, No.256, May 1996, pp.12-14. For 1997 elections see Shaul Bakhash, "Iran's Remarkable Election," *Journal of Democracy*, Vol.9, No.1, January 1998, pp.80-94.

one.[213] The first refers to elections plus civil liberties. These include autonomous civil society, separation between religion and state, protection for individual rights, and guarantees against arbitrary arrest and police brutality.[214] The latter is mainly focused on the process of coming to power through free elections. This distinction between the two types of democracy is relevant to the Iranian case. Samuel Huntington of Harvard University argues that the Islamic Republic is far from the Western liberal model but, "The Majlis is the liveliest parliament in the Middle East after the Israeli Knesset.[215]" Yahya Sadowski of Brookings Institution makes similar argument, "Iran is, in many ways, one of the most democratic societies in the Middle East. But, there is one problem: lack of civil liberties.[216]"

Examining the political process in Tehran since 1979 confirms their findings. On one side, since its inception, the Islamic regime has held reasonably free elections in which all adults 15 years and older, male and female, were allowed to vote. Also, it is important to point that for almost two decades the Majlis has never been dissolved and, unlike many other parliaments in the region, is not considered a "rubber stamp.[217]" Rather, the Majlis plays a significant role in making public policy.[218] On the other side, the Iranian democracy has its limits. First, the most powerful position, the faqih, is not chosen directly by the people. Second, it is true that the elections are, relatively speaking, free but the process of nomination is not. Candidates are screened for ideological purity by the Council of Guardians.[219] Third, the

---

[213] For example see Fareed Zakaria, "The Rise of Illiberal Democracy," *Foreign Affairs*, Vol.76, No.6, Nov/Dec 1997, pp.22-43.

[214] Larry Diamond, "Is the Third Wave over?" *Journal of Democracy*, Vol.7, No.3, July 1996, pp.20-37.

[215] Samuel Huntington, "After Twenty Years: The Future of The Third Wave," *Journal of Democracy*, Vol.8, No.4, October 1997, p.9.

[216] James Yahya Sadowski, "Prospects For Democracy In The Middle East: The Case Of Kuwait," *The Fletcher Forum of World Affairs*, Vol.21, No.1, Winter/Spring 1997, p.66.

[217] For example in June 1998 the Majlis dismissed the Interior Minister Abdullah Nouri, one of the closest allies to President Khatami.

[218] For a comprehensive study of the Majlis see Bahman Baktiari, *Parliamentary Politics In Revolutionary Iran*, Gainesville, FL: University Press of Florida, 1996.

[219] In the 1997 elections the Council of Guardians rejected all but 4 of the 238 presidential candidates.

guarantees against arbitrary arrest and police brutality are not vigorously enforced. Fourth, any criticism to the bases of the regime as they are defined by the clerics is almost not tolerated. Finally, political life in Tehran lacks the presence of recognized well-established political parties.[220]

In spite of all these limits of the Iranian democracy, the presidential election of 1997 should be seen as a significant step forward in the evolution toward more pluralism. Within the official ideological framework, votes were presented with different choices. Natiq Nouri, who was favored by the political/religious establishment, advocated conservatism. On the other side, Muhammad Khatami called for tolerance and reform. The fact that the latter won by almost 70 percent of the votes suggests that the majority of Iranians are yearning for personal and political freedom. It still is too early to make any judgement on the impact of Khatami's election on the evolution of the Islamic regime. However, three preliminary observations can shed some light on the direction the Islamic Republic is likely to take in the near future.

First, Khatami's previous experiences show a strong commitment to reform. During the 1960s and 1970s he wrote pamphlets criticizing the Shah's autocratic regime and became acquainted with Ayatollah Khomeini. Then he moved to Germany where he headed an Islamic Center. From 1982 to 1992 he served as Minister of Culture and Islamic Guidance where he built his reputation for moderation and tolerance.[221] Khatami was forced from his post by hard-liners who regarded him as too permissive.[222] Later he started teaching university courses about Islamic reform movements.[223] Finally, it is important to point out that since Khatami took office he has repeatedly confirmed that application of the rule of law remained his "greatest duty", his "pact with God", and his "promise to the people.[224]"

---

[220] A political parties law was passed in September 1981 that stipulated what constituted a political party and if and how it could functions. Still at the end of the 1990s, political parties do not exist.

[221] New York Times, "Moderate Leader Is Elected In Iran," May 25, 1997, p.10.

[222] Washington Post, "Moderate Iranian Wins," May 25, 1997, p.A28.

[223] New York Times, "Voice For Change," May 23, 1997, p.A10.

[224] Middle East Economic Digest, Vol.41, No.48, November 28, 1997, p.20.

Second, Khatami's cabinet appointments are mainly new faces with a reputation for competence and a somewhat less ideological outlook than their predecessors. The Foreign Minister, Kamal Kharrazi, played a central role in the 1990-91 negotiations that freed Western hostages held in Lebanon and served for eight years as Iran's Ambassador to the United Nations.[225] Minister of Culture and Islamic Guidance, Ataollah Mohajerani, has advocated greater cultural freedom and re-establishing relations with the United States.[226] Internal Security Minister, Qorbanali Najafabadi, replaced Ali Fallahin against whom Germany issued an arrest warrant for allegedly ordering political killing in Berlin.[227] Third, despite the euphoria which Khatami's election has incited, it is important to emphasize that he is not a dissident and has no intention of undermining the regime. The fact that his candidacy was approved by the Council of Guardians shows that he is considered well within the ideological boundaries accepted by the regime. Thus, Khatami should be seen as a reformer who wants to make the system work better. Finally, the president's power is restrained by other political institutions, particularly the Faqih.

To sum up, Khatami's tenure is likely to lead to a greater openness within the Islamic system. This process did not start with the 1997 presidential elections. Rather, the shift toward pluralistic political system as the unifying force of Iranian society began in the late 1980s with the death of Khomeini and the end of the eight-year war with Iraq. Under a platform initiated by then President Hashemi Rafsanjani, Iran began inching toward a more tolerant and less rigid political system. The election of Khatami not only confirms this trend, but demonstrates that the shift may be accelerating faster than previously understood. This move toward reform will be strongly influenced by how the Khatami's administration can meet the economic challenges facing the country.

---

[225] For a detailed discussion of Kharazi's opinions on a variety of foreign policy issues see *Middle East Insight*, Vol.13, No.1, November/December 1997, pp.34-39.

[226] *Middle East Monitor*, Vol.27, No.8, August 1997, p.60.

[227] Iran denied the charges.

ECONOMIC RE-CONSTRUCTION

Since the 1979 Revolution, profound changes have taken place in the Iranian economy in response to internal and external factors.[228] The political instability in the early months of the Revolution and the eight-year-war with Iraq which started in 1980 did not give Khomeini an opportunity to articulate and implement an Islamic economic model. Rather, it can be argued, the economic policy in most of the 1980s was, to a great extent, a response to the demands of the war with Iraq.[229] The Islamic regime endorsed private ownership but a large scale of modern industry as well as the entire banking and insurance sectors were nationalized shortly after the war started. This "transitional" stage came to an end in late 1980s with the cessation of hostilities in 1988 and the death of Khomeini the following year. The end of the war incited expectations that all resources will be allocated to economic prosperity. No more need for sacrifices. The departure of Ayatollah meant that the regime lost the last authority who probably would have been able to ask his countrymen for further patience.[230] Under these conditions the post-war Iranian economy started a new phase. Three factors have had (and will continue to have) significant impact on the development of the economy: population growth and structure, economic management, and the oil sector.

Demographic change: Immediately after the revolution many conservative clerics declared contraceptives to be a Western weapon used to reduce the number of Muslims and weaken Muslim nations.[231] As a result, the

---

[228] For a thorough analysis of the Iranian economy since the Revolution see Jahangir Amuzegar, *Iran's Economy Under The Islamic Republic*, London: I.B.Tauris, 1993. And, Anoushiravan Ehteshami, After Khomeini: *The Iranian Second Republic*, London: Routledge, 1995.

[229] In other words, "The Iranian economy in the 1980s can be characterized as a managed war economy rather than a centrally-planned command economy of the Eastern European type." See Massoud Karshenas and M. Hashem Pesaran, "Economic Reform And The Reconstruction Of The Iranian Economy," *Middle East Journal*, Vol.49, No.1, Winter 1995, p.97.

[230] Henner Furtig, p.36.

[231] Geoffrey Kemp and Janice Gross Stein, "Enduring Sources Of Conflict In The Persian Gulf Region: Predicting Shocks To The System," in, G. Kemp & J. Stein, (eds.), *Powder Keg In The Middle East*, Lanham, MD: Rowman & Littlefield, 1995, p.9.

population growth rate soared to 3.4 percent.[232] This population explosion has altered the demographic structure of the country.[233] In the second half of the 1990s, it is estimated that 45 percent of the population is under 14 years old.[234] This huge number of young people poses tremendous challenge for the government to provide them with jobs. Thus, unemployment and underemployment have been an important feature of the Iranian economy for several years and are likely to remain so for the foreseeable future.[235] This socio-economic problem, among others, incited the Iranian government to launch an ambitious program for economic reform in the early 1990s.

Economic management: As has been suggested above, the end of the war with Iraq and the beginning of Rafsanjani's presidency provided an opportunity to address the economic problems. The main objective was a general improvement of the quality of life of the population. Two important external developments encouraged the government to pursue a structural adjustment strategy in dealing with the critical economic situation. First, the weakening and final collapse of the Soviet Union proved the failure of the state-led economic model. This approach was adopted in the Islamic Republic in most of the first decade of the revolution in order to achieve self sufficiency by expanding the role of the public sector and reducing the economic and financial interaction between Iran and the global market. In other words, by the late 1980s it became clear that the populist economic policy was not working. Second, the Iraqi invasion and occupation of Kuwait in August 1990 took the oil of the two countries off the international market and consequently pushed oil prices up. This added an unexpected extra five billion dollars to Iran's treasury (in 1989 oil revenues were $11 billion, in 1990 they climbed to $16 billion.[236]) Equally important, the neutral stand Tehran took during the crisis improved its image both in the region and in the international scene. The

---

[232] *United Nations Development Program,* Human Development Report, New York: Oxford University Press, 1997, table 22, p.194.

[233] Later the government endorsed a birth-control policy.

[234] Central Intelligence Agency, *World Factbook,* Washington DC: United States Printing Office, 1998, p.227.

[235] It is estimated that the unemployment rate in Iran was over 30 percent in 1995. See Central Intelligence Agency, *World Factbook,* Washington DC: US Government Printing Office, 1998, p.222.

[236] Central Intelligence Agency, *Handbook of International Economic Statistics,* Washington DC: United States Government Printing Office, 1996, table 51, p.94.

Rafsanjani's government, with its emphasize on ending the country's isolation, tried to take full advantage of this positive environment.

It was against this background that the First Five-Year Plan was initiated and implemented covering the period from 1989 to 1993. The Plan provided a framework for economic liberalization including privatizing public enterprises, reducing subsidies, lifting price control, promoting free trade, and encouraging private and foreign investment.[237] In short, the Plan sought to implement a structural adjustment program as described by the World Bank and the International Monetary Fund (IMF). An important manifestation of this new direction was the creation of several free trade zones. These include Qeshm, Kish, Chahbahar, Sirjan, Sarakhs, and Bandar Enzeli. They all offer tax holidays, exemption from customs duties, and other incentives to attract private and foreign investments.

This "Rafsanjani's Perestroika", as it is often called, had been short-lived and hesitant. Since the late 1993 and early 1994, Rafsanjani's reform efforts had slowed down and almost came to a halt. Given the political climate inside Iran and in the Gulf region, very few foreign investors brought in their money. Instead, the government had to rely on foreign borrowing which resulted in $23.4 billion foreign debt in very short time.[238] Moreover, little efforts were made to reform the huge bureaucracy for fear of further aggravating the unemployment problem. Finally, Economic liberalization policies fuelled inflation and disparity in incomes. Most severely affected were lower-income and middle-class or fixed-income households.[239] These social classes represent the main constituency for the revolution. The clerical regime could not afford

---

[237] In 1991 more than 250 Western, Asian, and Arab oil ministers attended the first international conference held in Iran since the revolution. The meeting, "Oil and Gas in the 1990s: Prospect For Cooperation," was addressed by President Rafsanjani, Foreign Minister Velayati, Oil Minister Aqazadeh, and Finance Minister Nourbakhsh. All of them called for greater economic and political cooperation with the West and closer ties with the Gulf states. See Youssef Ibrahim, "Iran's Leaders Ask Wide Cooperation And Ties To West," New York Times, May 28, 1991, P.A1.

[238] In 1989 Iran's total debt stood at $6.5 billion. Four years later, 1993, it reached $23.4 billion. See The World Bank, *World Debt Tables*, Washington DC, 1996, p.226.

[239] Hooshang Amirahmadi, "Iran's Development: Evaluation And Challenges," *Third World Quarterly*, Vol.17, No.1, March 1998, p.138.

to alienate them. Not surprisingly, the IMF mentions "insufficient commitment" as a crucial reason for the slow reform efforts.[240]

The First Five-Year Plan ended in 1993 and the second one started in 1995. The two plans are very similar in their goal to introduce market mechanism and push for more integration into the global economy. However, the second plan focuses more on social justice in an attempt to alleviate the pain of the lower class. In addition, more attention is given to repay foreign debt. This was made easier in 1995 and 1996 due to an unexpected rise in oil prices. Thus, the better economic performance in these two years can be explained less by a rational economic planning and more by exogenous factor. Finally, President Khatami's policy is strongly in support of continuing and renewing efforts to reform the economy. Significant efforts have already been made in the most important sector-oil.

The Oil Sector: Oil revenues are the main source of Iran's foreign currency earnings. Over the last two decades, however, this vital economic sector has suffered from severe problems mainly for political reasons. The wide-spread political turmoil in the late 1970s and the new regime' desire to reduce the country's dependence on oil and Western companies resulted in a substantial reduction in production. In 1978, Iran's oil production stood at 5.2 million barrel per day (b/d), by 1981 it dropped to only 1.3 billion b/d.[241] In the rest of the decade, the country's production and export capabilities were frequent subject to the Iraqi attacks. Still, the government managed to slowly increase production. Since the early 1990s, Iran has not spared any efforts to update and modernize its oil sector. Given the large reserves, the Islamic Republic has the resources to raise its production capacity. The United States Department of Energy projects that Iran's oil production capacity will rise from 3.9 million b/d in 1995 to 5.9 million b/d by 2015.[242]

However, the major obstacle for Tehran to achieve this goal is the American policy of blocking any foreign investment in the Iranian oil sector. In order to overcome Washington's containment policy the Islamic regime has

---

[240] International Monetary Fund, *World Economic Outlook*, Washington DC, May 1996, p.101.

[241] Energy Information Administration, *International Petroleum Statistics Report*, Washington DC: US Government Printing Office, August 1997, table 4.1a, p.38.

[242] Energy Information Administration, *International Energy Outlook*, Washington DC: US Government Printing Office, 1997, table A40, p.157.

sought to provide financial incentives to lure foreign investment. Among others, three important measures have been recently considered. First, "buy-back" scheme in which international oil companies will be reimbursed for their investment through subsequent oil production. This arrangement permits Iran to get around constitutional opposition to the entry of foreign firms into its energy projects. Second, lifting of the 49 percent shareholding ceiling for foreign partners in joint ventures to 99 percent.[243] Third, until now foreign investment has been sought to boost only offshore oil fields not onshore ones. Recently the Majlis is considering legislation to open the latter to international companies.[244] In the closing years of the 1990s, it seems that these incentives have succeeded in luring foreign investors from France, Russia, Malaysia, Canada, and others.

Still, given the prominent role oil plays in the Iranian economy both at present and in the foreseeable future, more needs to be done. In order to fully utilize its hydrocarbon resources and sustain its economic growth, the Islamic Republic needs freer access to foreign investment and advanced techniques of production.

CONCLUSION AND POLICY IMPLICATIONS

The presidential elections of May 1997 and the ascent to power of Khatami provide an important opportunity to reflect on where the Islamic Republic stands, what direction it might take under the Khatami's administration, and how other countries should respond. After almost two decades in power, there are no signs that the Islamic regime is about to collapse. Most likely it will remain in power for the foreseeable future. However, Iran at the end of the 1990s looks different from the one of 1979. The change is real. Under Rafsanjani's administration an attempt was made to introduce economic reform and improve relations with foreign countries. The outcome was neither complete success nor complete failure. But there is no denying that important steps were taken towards moderation.

---

[243] *Middle East Economic Digest*, vol.41, No.47, November 21, 1997, p.11.

[244] Bob Tippee, "Iran Enacting Reforms To Lure E&D Investment," *Oil & Gas Journal*, Vol.96, No.2, January 12, 1998, p.24.

Khatami's previous experience in government and the political initiatives he has taken since he became president suggest that his administration will remain on the path his predecessor had taken. More important is the fact that the voters (all Iranians, men and women, age 15 and over) were presented with two choices: one stood for moderation and the other for conservatism. In free elections (something not very common in this part of the world) the majority of Iranians chose the candidate who called for more freedom.

The contention of this chapter is that over the next few years there will probably not be dramatic change in Iranian policy on the surface. However, Khatami's main contribution might be in deepening and enlarging the reform programs Rafsanjani introduced. This change will be slow, gradual and, sometimes, unnoticed, but it will have a long-term impact. A market economy and integration in the international system would consolidate democracy and civil liberties in Iran and would improve the chances of peaceful relations between the Islamic Republic and its neighbors.

Foreign powers should not take a "wait-and-see" approach. Instead, dialogue and engagement would help to influence the direction of change. There will be many setbacks, but the stakes are high. The stability of Iran is crucial to the security of oil supplies from both the Persian Gulf and the Caspian Basin.

Chapter 8

GULF SECURITY: RETROSPECT AND PROSPECT

Less than a decade after the official British withdrawal from the Persian Gulf in 1971, the security system in the region has confronted tremendous challenges. First, the violent overthrow of the Pahlavi dynasty and its replacement by the Islamic Republic created new regional order. This was shortly followed by the long eight-year war between Iran and Iraq. In 1988 Tehran's military capabilities were immensely reduced due to the great losses the country had suffered at the hands of the Iraqis particularly in the last year of the fighting. This apparent weakness of the region's most populous state did not produce a stable security environment. Rather, the then one-million Iraqi army invaded Kuwait. The Gulf War dealt a heavy blow to the second most populous country in the region-Iraq. Thus, by the early 1990s, the two regional giants were militarily (and economically) weakened by the outcome of the two wars.

Like the Iran-Iraq war, the war to liberate Kuwait has failed to create a permanent peace in the Persian Gulf. Put differently, in the closing years of the twentieth century the Persian Gulf states are still searching for an adequate answer to their security dilemma. One explanation for this lack of solid and permanent peace in the region is the disagreement on the source of threat. This chapter will examine several real and potential challenges to the regional security system. These include the demographic composition and its impact on arms race, border-disputes, the threat from Iran, the threat from Iraq, and the proliferation of weapons of mass destruction (WMD). The main contention is that a permanent peace in the Persian Gulf should not be built on a zero-sum perception. In other words, the gains of one country should not be at the expense of another one. Instead, all the eight regional states should strengthen their economic, cultural, and political ties in order to create an integrated Gulf system. Integration and cooperation, not confrontation, need to be emphasized in order to establish a strong foundation for a stable security system in the Persian Gulf.

DEMOGRAPHIC COMPOSITION

One of the main reasons for the consistent tension in the Persian Gulf is the asymmetrical distribution of manpower and wealth as the following table demonstrates.[245].

Table I
Disparity in Wealth and Military Power between the Gulf States
(1996)

Country	1	2	3	4
Bahrain	15,321	11.0	476	5.5
Kuwait	21,875	15.3	2,218	12.9
Oman	10,078	43.5	955	15.6
Qatar	18,403	11.8	1,334	10.2
Saudi Arabia	9,338	162.5	1,030	12.8
UAE	16,000	64.5	830	5.2
Iran	5,766	513.0	49	5.0
Iraq	3,159	382.5	56	8.3

1 = ppp is real GDP per capita
2 = numbers in armed forces in thousands of people
3 = defense expenditure per capita in US dollars
4 = defense expenditure as percentage of GDP
Source: United Nations Development Program, *Human Development Report*, New York: Oxford University Press, 1997, pp.146-147. And, International Institute for Strategic Studies, *The Military Balance*, New York: Oxford University Press, 1997, p.294.

---

[245]For a detailed discussion see Gawdat Bahgat, "Military Security and Political Stability in the Gulf," *Arab Studies Quarterly*, Vol.17, No.4, Fall 1995 pp.55-70; "Regional Peace and Stability in the Gulf," *Security Dialogue*, Vol.26, No.3, 1995b, pp.317-330; and "Gulf Security and Western Policy," *The International Spectator*, Vol.31, No.3, July-September 1996, pp.39-49.

The figures show the huge imbalance between militarily weak states sitting on an extremely valuable resources and their not so-rich but much more powerful two neighbors. In addition to this demographic disadvantage, the six Gulf monarchies have never endorsed the idea of having a large and professional army.[246] This is a rational concern given the military's penchant for attempting to overthrow monarchies in the Middle East.[247] No wonder most of these states have small armies that are fitted more to serve as a police force to maintain domestic stability and less as a professional army to defend the country from an external aggression. In an attempt to overcome this shortage of manpower the six monarchies have sought to coordinate their defense policies. The great illustration of this strategy is the creation of the Gulf Cooperation Council shortly after the outbreak of the Iran-Iraq war.[248] Another significant step was the efforts to increase the joint military forces known as Peninsula Shield and stationed at Hafr al-Batin in northeastern Saudi Arabia in the aftermath of the Gulf War.[249]

Still the most important policy adopted by the six monarchies to overcome their demographic disadvantage has been to rely on buying the most advanced military technology.[250] According to Stockholm International Peace Research Institute (SIPRI) Saudi Arabia has been the leading recipient of major

---

[246] See Hamad Khatani, "The Preservation of Civilian Rule in Saudi Arabia," pp.53-72, in Constantine P. Danopoulos, (ed.), *Civilian Rule in the Developing World: Democracy on the March?*, Boulder, CO: Westview Press, 1992.

[247] Rlin G. Mainuddin, Joseph R. Aicher, and Jeffrey M. Elliot, "From Alliance to Collective Security: Rethinking the Gulf Cooperation Council," *Middle East Policy*, Vol.4, No.3, March 1996, p.41.

[248] For a thorough analysis of the circumstances under which the Gulf Cooperation Council was created see Ralph H. Magnus, "The GCC and Security: The Enemy without and the Enemy within," *Journal of South Asian and Middle Eastern Studies*, Vol.20, No.3, Spring 1997, pp.72-94. And Joseph A. Kechichian, *Security Efforts in the Arab World: A Brief Examination of Four Regional Organizations*, Santa Monica, CA: RAND, 1993.

[249] See Gregory Gause, *Oil Monarchies: Domestic and Security Challenges in the Arab Gulf States*, New York: Council on Foreign Relations Press, 1994 particularly chapter 5, pp.119-145.

[250] For one of the best studies on arms race in the Middle East see Yahya M. Sadowski, Scuds or Butter? The Political Economy of Arms Control in the Middle East, Washington D.C.: The Brookings Institution, 1993.

conventional weapons in the world since the early 1990s.[251] The other five Gulf monarchies have also made substantial arms purchases. This huge money spent on armament in conjunction with the stagnant oil prices have contributed to financial pressure on the public treasuries. In an attempt to alleviate this pressure some of these Arab Gulf states introduced what is known as offset program.[252] According to this arrangement the foreign firms which export armaments to the Gulf monarchies are required to invest directly as joint minority partners in non-oil sector, export-related enterprises within the recipient states. This will enable Gulf economies to acquire foreign direct investment and in turn will facilitate the development of non-petroleum, export based industries in addition to the modernization of military equipment.[253] It still is too early to provide any credible assessment of the offset programs.

Regardless of the impact of these arrangements, there is no doubt that the six Arab Gulf states will maintain high level of military expenditure in the twenty-first century. Two reasons lay the ground for this prediction. First, this highly-advanced military equipment increases the defense capabilities of the Arab Gulf states. Second, and probably more important, these billions of dollars spent on armament cement the connection between the defense of the Gulf states and the prosperity and well-being of Western economies. Put differently, increasingly arms industry in Washington, London, and Paris depends on exporting weapons to the Gulf monarchies. Inevitably, the interests of the two sides have become intertwined. If one sinks the other follows. Thus, it can be concluded that this very high military spending since the early 1990s has enhanced the protection of the six Arab Gulf states from any aggression by either Iran or Iraq. However, the impact of this policy on a potential conflict between the six monarchies is uncertain. Such conflicts can be incited by disagreements on the boundaries separating these states.

---

[251] Stockholm International Peace Research Institute, SIPRI Yearbook: Armaments, Disarmament and International Security, New York: Oxford University Press, 1997, p.272.

[252] For example see Amin Badr El-Din, "The Offsets Program in the United Arab Emirates," Middle East Policy, Vol.5, No.1, January 1997, pp.120-123.

[253] Jamal S. Al-Suwaidi, "Gulf Security and the Iranian Challenge," Security Dialogue, Vol.27, No.3, September 1996, p.286.

BORDER-DISPUTES

The concepts of nation-state, of territorial sovereignty, and of fixed linear frontiers are Western ones[254], which have no roots in most of the Persian Gulf societies. Most of the present-day borders between states in the region have their origins in the international arrangements arising from the dismemberment of the Ottoman Empire at the end of World War I. Since then four forces have shaped the political map of the region and contributed to some of the unsettled border disputes. These forces are tribalism, the perception of the state in Islam, the British legacy, and the discovery of oil.

For hundreds of years the principal social and political unit in the Persian Gulf society had been the tribe.[255] Tribalism still is an important individual and group identity in modern Gulf states. Several ruling families in the region stemmed from the tribal federations of eastern Saudi Arabia-the Aniza in Kuwait, Bahrain and Qatar and the Qawasim in the United Arab Emirates.[256] The consolidation and expansion of their rule depended on their ability to dominate or accommodate other tribes. For centuries these tribes roamed the desert without any restrictions on their movement. This persistent of tribal identity and the absence or weakening of national identity did not contradict with the teaching of Islam. Islamic political thinking subscribes more to the notion of "umma," the community of believers, and less to the concept of nation state. In Islamic history Sovereignty was concerned primarily with community and not with territory.[257] This secondary interest in the territorial

---

[254] Julian Walker, "The United Arab Emirates and Oman Frontiers," pp.173-183, in Clive H. Schofield and Richard N. Schofield, (eds.), London: Routledge, 1994.

[255] For a discussion of the tribe as a political unit in the Middle East in general see Philip S Khoury and Joseph Kostiner, (eds.), *Tribes and State Formation in the Middle East*, Berkeley, CA: University of California Press, 1990. For an analysis of the role of tribes in the creation of Gulf states see J.E. Peterson, "Tribes and Politics in Eastern Arabia," *Middle East Journal*, Vol.31, No.3, Summer 1977, pp.297-312.

[256] Burke's Royal Families of the World, Vol.2: *Africa and the Middle East*, London: Burke's Peerage LTD, 1980.

[257] George Joffe, "Territory, State and Nation in the Middle East and North Africa," p.3, in Clive H. Schofield and Richard N. Schofield, (eds.), *The Middle East and North Africa*, London: Routledge, 1994.

configuration of the state has changed with the increased Western presence in the region particularly the British authority since the late nineteenth century.

Probably it is safe to state that Britain, more than any other foreign power, played a decisive role in drawing the boundaries between the Gulf states. Two significant episodes illustrate the impact of the British legacy. First in 1922 a conference was held in uqair, Saudi Arabia. Two-thirds of the land claimed by Kuwait at that time was awarded to Saudi Arabia by the British authority.[258] In addition, two "neutral zones[259]" were created one between Iraq and Saudi Arabia and the other between the latter and Kuwait. In the two zones, tribes from the three states enjoyed equal rights to water and pasture. The Iraq-Saudi Neutral Zone was partitioned by agreements in 1975 and 1981. Since then the frontiers between the two states have been stabilized.[260] The Kuwait-Saudi Neutral Zone was divided into equal shares and the modified borders between the two states were delimited in a series of agreements in the 1960s.[261] However, the two sides have failed to agree on the islands of Qaruh and Umm el-Maradim located off the coast of the northern part of the zone.[262] The other episode occurred more than three decades later and is known as Buraimi crisis. Acting on behalf of Abu Dhabi and Oman, British forces forcibly evicted the Saudi army from the oasis of Buraimi. The British government then divided the area between Oman and Abu Dhabi. It took the kingdom several years to acknowledge its new borders with the two states.

These British efforts to define the borders between the Gulf states were, at least partly, incited by the discovery of oil. Shortly after World War I petroleum concessions were obtained for Iraq, and some of the other Arab

---

[258] Rosemarie Said Zahlan, *The Making of the Modern Gulf States: Kuwait, Bahrain, Qatar, The United Arab Emirates and Oman*, London: Unwin Hyman, 1989, p.17.

[259] These are usually agreed upon when territorial disputes between neighboring states reach deadlock and generally involve a partial surrender of sovereignty over the area in question.

[260] During the Gulf crisis (1990-91) the validity of the 1981 agreement was not questioned by either Iraq or Saudi Arabia.

[261] Richard Schofield, "Borders and Territoriality in the Gulf and the Arabian Peninsula during the Twentieth Century," p.45 in Richard Schofield, (ed.), *Territorial Foundations of the Gulf States*, London: UCL Press, 1994.

[262] At the end of the 1990s the islands remain under Kuwaiti control but Saudi Arabia has never abandoned its claim to sovereignty over them.

Gulf states. The exploration agreements were secured under the assumption that the rulers enjoyed sovereignty over well-defined territories. Thus, it can be concluded that oil discovery accelerated the process of boundary delineation in the Gulf region. Still, in the closing years of the twentieth century some of these disagreements over the configuration of each state have not been settled. One of the most serious and most enduring border-disputes is the conflict between Bahrain and Qatar over the Hawar Islands.

The problem first became apparent in 1938 when the ruler of Bahrain claimed the Hawar Islands purely for the purposes of oil exploration.[263] This claim was immediately rejected by the ruler of Qatar on the basis that the islands are located within its territorial waters. Britain, then the dominant power in the region, endorsed the Bahraini claims. In the aftermath of the British official withdrawal in 1971 Saudi Arabia resumed the responsibility of mediating the dispute between the two parties. The Saudi efforts did not succeed to bring Bahrain and Qatar to agree on a satisfactory solution. Thus, in July 1991 the latter instituted proceedings at the international Court of Justice. Being in control of the islands, Bahrain has been reluctant to accept the court jurisdiction. It is unlikely that any settlement reached by the court will completely satisfy either side. The dispute over the Hawar Islands between Bahrain and Qatar is likely to endure well into the twenty-first century.

In closing, it is important to point out that most of the treaties signed between the six Gulf monarchies apply only to the land boundaries. Extensive efforts need to be invested to agree on maritime boundary delimitation. Furthermore, the territorial conflicts with Iran and Iraq add to the regional instability.

IS IRAN A THREAT?

Regardless of the political orientation in Tehran, Iran has always enjoyed a "special" status among the Persian Gulf states. Unlike its Gulf neighbors, the majority of Iranians are not Arabs. They are Persian, Azerbaijani, Gilaki and

---

[263] John B. Allcock, Guy Arnold, Alan J. Day, D. S. Lewis, Lorimer Poultney, Roland Rance, D. J. Sagar, (eds.), *Border and Territorial Disputes*, London: Longman, 1992, p.366.

Mazandarani, Kurd, and others. This difference in ethnicity is offset by the fact that Iran's population is larger than that of all the other seven Arab Gulf states combined. This demographic imbalance between the two sides of the Gulf is further complicated by sectarian division. Iran is the only country in the Gulf where Shi'is are in power. In Iraq and Bahrain the Shi'is are the majority but the two governments are dominated by Sunnis. In the rest of the Gulf the Shi'is are minority. These differences between the two sides have shaped their relations for long time. For centuries most of the Arab Gulf states (and the rest of the Middle East) were under control by foreign powers (i.e. Ottoman and British empires). The relations between these foreign powers and the ruling dynasties in Iran were, for the most part, characterized by suspicion and hostility. In the twentieth century the British legacy had left two major territorial disputes between Iran and its Arab neighbors. The first one is about Bahrain and the other is related to the three islands (Abu Musa, Greater Tunb, and Lesser Tunb) between Iran and the United Arab Emirates.

The first Iranian claim to Bahrain during the Pahlavi period was made in the late 1920s.[264] Since then Iran refused to recognize Bahrain as a British-protected sheikdom.[265] The dispute escalated further in the mid 1950s following the passing of a bill by the Iranian parliament declaring Bahrain as the 14th Iranian province.[266] In the late 1960s, however, the Iranian attitude became more conciliatory. At the request of both Iran and Britain, the United Nations Secretary-General appointed a special representative to visit Bahrain in order to ascertain the wishes of its population in regard to its future status. This was followed by an endorsement of Bahrain's independence by the Iranian parliament and government.[267] Shortly after the overthrow of the Shah

---

[264] Rosemarie Said Zahlan, "King Abd Al-Aziz's Changing Relationship with the Gulf States During the 1930s," p.64, in Tim Niblock, (ed.), *State, Society and Economy in Saudi Arabia*, New York: ST. Martin's Press, 1982.

[265] Bahrain was under Iranian (Persian) domination for almost two centuries (from 1602 to 1783). This ended when Al-Khalifa, the current ruling family invaded the island.

[266] For a detailed discussion of this period see Alvin J. Cottrell, (ed.), *The Persian Gulf States: A General Survey*, Baltimore: Johns Hopkins University, 1980, particularly chapter 4 by Malcolm Yapp, "British Policy in the Persian Gulf," pp.70-100.

[267] Fred Halliday, *Arabia Without Sultans: A Political Survey of Instability in the Arab World*, New York: Vintage Books, 1974, p.469.

in 1979 Ayatollah Ruhani, a leading figure in the Islamic revolution renewed Iranian claim to Bahrain.[268] These claims were strongly rejected by the Bahraini government and other Arab states. Since then Tehran has not reasserted these claims. Thus, it seems that the Bahrain-Iran territorial dispute has been settled. This conclusion does not apply to the one regarding the three islands between Iran and the United Arab Emirates.

Indeed, the two territorial disputes are related. Some observers believe that in return for relaxing the Shah's position on Bahrain he consolidated his demand for the three islands (Abu Musa and the two Tunbs) with little, if any, British opposition.[269] In late November 1971, before the proclamation of the United Arab Emirates as a new state, Iranian troops occupied the three islands. This development was accompanied by strong statements from Iranian officials confirming the historical and legal rights of Tehran over the disputed islands. Also, the Iranian advance was based on agreement between Iran and the Sharjah (one of the seven emirates composing the UAE). Expectedly, the Arab reaction was absolute rejection and condemnation of Tehran's seizure of the islands.[270] This, however, had little impact on the dispute for most of the following two decades. In 1992 Iran confirmed its authority over the disputed islands by preventing foreigners who did not hold an Iranian visa from entering Abu Musa. This was followed by taking more measure to expand Tehran's control over the island.

There are three explanations for this persistent Iranian interest in the three islands: security, oil, and domestic politics. The three islands are located on the Strait of Hormuz where most of the Gulf oil is shipped through. The control of these islands has given Iran an important strategic advantage. In addition, any potential oil discoveries inshore or offshore would add economic benefit. Finally, the leaders of the Islamic Republic can not afford to look

---

[268] John B. Allcock, Guy Arnold, Alan J. Day, D. S. Lewis, Lorimer Poultney, Roland Rance, D. J. Sagar, *Border and Territorial Disputes*, London: Longman, 1992, p.365.

[269] Anthony H. Cordesman, *The Gulf and the Search for Strategic Stability*, Boulder, CO: Westview Press, 1984, p.149.

[270] For an Iranian account of the dispute see the detailed study by Hooshang Amirahmadi, (ed.), Small Islands, Big Politics: The Tonbs and Abu Musa in the Persian Gulf, New York: ST. Martin Press, 1996. For a pro-Arab account see Dan Caldwell, "Flashpoints in the Gulf: Abu Musa and the Tunb Islands," *Middle East Policy*, Vol.4, No.3, March 1996, pp.50-57.

weaker than the predecessor regime. They can not give up the islands which the Shah "restored" to the Iranian domain. Regardless of these incentives, the rulers of the UAE with support from the other Gulf monarchies have been calling on Iran to withdraw from the islands. Given the fact that the UAE is not militarily strong enough to force Iran to change its course, no change is expected. Instead, a war of words between the two sides is likely to endure well into the new millennium.

It is important to understand these territorial disputes over Bahrain and the three islands in the context of the evolution of the Iranian-Arab relations. The Pahlavi regime enjoyed close cooperation with the Gulf monarchies. The two sides advocated a conservative and pro-Western policy. The Iranian participation in defeating the leftist rebellion in Dhafor, Oman (from mid 1960s to mid 1970s) can be seen as an illustration of this close cooperation and common interests between the two sides.[271] However, given the Arab suspicion in Iran's intentions, there was no formal security alliance in the Gulf.

Ayatollah Khomeini's rise to power and the rhetoric of exporting the revolution deepened the gap between Iran and its Arab neighbors. Not surprisingly, for most of the 1980s the Arab monarchies supported Iraq in its war against Iran. The end of the fighting and Rafsanjani's rise to power opened a new chapter in the Gulf politics. Tehran's neutrality during the 1990-91 crisis earned it goodwill among the six Gulf states. Taking advantage of this new political environment, Rafsanjani engaged in a series of confidence-building exercises with the Gulf rulers. Tehran's new regional policy was described as "Rafsanjani's pragmatic peace.[272]" According to this strategy, the Islamic Republic's behavior toward its neighbors has been guided more by economic interests and less with religious dogma since the early 1990s.

Khatami's regional orientation should be seen as a continuation of a trend started under his predecessor Rafsanjani. The new president made improving relations with Iran's neighbors a cornerstone in his foreign policy. In the

---

[271] A leftist movement called the Popular Front for the Liberation of Oman launched a guerrilla war against Al Said, the ruling family in Oman, This revolt was backed by another leftist regime that came to power Aden, South Yemen in 1969. The revolt was finally crushed in the mid 1970s with the aid of Iranian, Saudi, Jordanian, and British troops.

[272] The term is borrowed from R. K. Ramazani, "The Emerging Arab-Iranian Rapprochement: Towards an Integrated U.S. Policy in the Middle East?" *Middle East Policy*, Vol.6, No.1, June 1998, p.47.

closing years of the twentieth century several signs point out to the Arab/Iranian rapprochement. These include the decision to raise the diplomatic relations between Iran and Bahrain to the ambassadorial level for the first time in nearly twenty years and the high-level Arab turnout in the Islamic Conference Organization (ICO) summit held in Tehran in December 1997[273]. Another significant step was the well-publicized visit by Iran's former President Rafsanjani to Saudi Arabia in early 1998 and the signing of several agreements of economic cooperation between the two countries. A major reason for this rapprochement between the Arab Gulf states and Iran is the deadlock in the Palestinian-Israeli peace process. The election of Benjamin Netanyahu in 1996 brought the negotiations to a halt. Particularly important for both the Saudis and the Iranians is the Israeli Prime Minister's plan to expand control over Jerusalem.

This process of building confidence between Iran and the Gulf monarchies has been accompanied by similar, but slower, steps to improve relations with Iraq. During the Islamic summit the Iraqi Vice President, Taha Yasin Ramadan, was the most senior official to visit Iran since the revolution. This was followed by significant exchange of prisoners of war between the two countries and an agreement in 1998 to permit Iranian pilgrims to resume direct travel to Shi'i shrines in Iraq for the first time since 1980.[274]

Naturally, this process of improving relations between Iran and its Arab Gulf neighbors has not hindered Tehran's efforts to enhance its defense capability. Unlike Iraq, the Islamic Republic has been under less scrutiny by the international community to modernize its armed forces for most of the 1990s. In addition, Tehran has encountered fewer constraints building up its defense industry in order to reduce dependence on external arms suppliers.[275] More important, over the last several years Tehran has developed carefully focused military capabilities.[276] More attention has been given to strengthening the navy. Many observers believe that Iran's land forces do not pose a threat

---

[273] In this summit Crown Prince Abdullah represented the kingdom and was the most eminent member of the Saudi royal family to have visited Iran since the establishment of the Islamic Republic.

[274] BBC News on line, "Progress for Iranian Pilgrims," July 8, 1998.

[275] For more details on Iran's arms industry see Anoushiravan Ehteshami, *After Khomeini: The Iranian Second Republic*, London: Routledge, 1995, pp.182-187.

[276] Anthony H. Cordesman, *"The Changing Military Balance in the Gulf,"* Middle East Policy, Vol.6, No.1, June 1998, p.25.

beyond its borders. But the naval force, with a sea mine-capability and fast patrol boats fitted with missiles, could disrupt shipping in the Gulf.[277]

This potential Iranian threat to navigation in the Gulf is restrained by two factors. On one side Tehran's operational naval forces (including the three kilo-class submarines it bought from Russia in the early 1990s) are no match for the American Fifth Fleet which continues to exercise in the Gulf with no prospects for leaving any time soon. On the other side, unlike Iraq and Saudi Arabia, which can choose from a variety of pipelines, all Iranian crude oil is exported from the Kharg island terminal located in the northern Gulf. Put differently, disruption of free navigation in the Gulf would be suicidal to the country's economy.

Thus, it can be stated that an Iranian move to disrupt oil shipment from the Gulf is highly unlikely. Simply stated, Tehran lacks both the military power and the political will to take such action. This conclusion is reinforced by the improved relations between the Iranian and Arabian sides of the Gulf. Several issues will continue to shape these relations well into the new millennium.[278] These include religion, water, oil, and other political developments. Islam is an important component of the legitimacy of the political systems in both Riyadh and Tehran as well as in the rest of the Gulf states (to a lesser extent). Iran is the current chair of the Islamic Conference Organization (1997-2000) and the kingdom presents itself as the protector of the Islamic holy sites. This can incite either cooperation or conflict between the two states. In addition, the six Gulf monarchies suffer from a severe water shortage. Iran is in a position to provide an immense volume of water in a cheap price to the region. In the early 1990s Iran and Qatar negotiated an agreement to bring Karun river water from the former to the latter.[279] Furthermore, there are several oil and gas fields in the Persian Gulf that Iran and the Arab Gulf states are either jointly exploiting or have agreed to do so in the future. The list includes Foruzan (with Saudi Arabia), Mobarak and Dalan

---

[277] For example see The International Institute for Strategic Studies, *The Military Balance*, New York: Oxford University Press, 1997, p.116.

[278] For a thorough analysis of these issues see Shahram Chubin and Charles Tripp, *Iran-Saudi Arabia Relations and Regional Order*, Adelphi Paper No.304, New York: Oxford University Press for the International Institute for Strategic Studies, 1996.

[279] For more details see Andrew Whitley and Katherine Gallagher, "Karun River Politics," *Middle East Insight*, Vol.10, No.5, July-August 1995, pp.33-35.

Kangan (with the UAE), Hengam (with Oman), and the Southern Pars (with Qatar).[280] More to the point, oil is the main source of public revenues in all these Gulf states. As has been demonstrated in 1997 and 1998, a drop in oil prices can sharply hurt their economies and force them to coordinate their production policy. Moreover both Iran and the Arab Gulf states have found themselves on the same side in other recent political issues such as opposing the Israeli/Turkish military alliance, confronting the Israeli expansion in Jerusalem, supporting the Muslims in Bosnia and, since the late 1990s, attempting to end the civil war in Afghanistan. Finally, Iran is perceived by some of the Arab Gulf states as a counterweight to Iraq.

These issues can facilitate cooperation or incite conflict between Iran and the Arab monarchies in the next several decades. It is impossible to provide a credible prediction on what direction the political leadership on the two sides of the Gulf will choose. If the past is any guide, most likely the future of the Iranian/Arab relations in the twenty-first century will continue to be a mixture of cooperation and competition. To some extent, this will be influenced by the developments in the other Gulf state-Iraq.

IRAQ'S GULF POLICY-WHAT IS NEXT?

Since 1980 Iraq has been in conflict with one or more of its Gulf neighbors. Indeed these troubling relations can be traced back several decades ago. A major reason for this legacy of violence and instability is the Iraqi perception of injustice. Over the years many Iraqi leaders expressed dissatisfaction with the configuration of their country. They believe that Britain, intentionally, gave Iraq the smallest outlet on the Persian Gulf (58 km) and made the country dependent on the goodwill of its neighbors in exporting its oil and in receiving its needs of water. No wonder, the Iraqi leaders have not missed any opportunity to "correct" this perceived injustice. In 1960s and 1970s the Iraqi efforts to challenge the territorial status quo were contained by unfavored regional and international environments.

---

[280] Asghar Ja'Fari Valdani, "Iran and the Persian Gulf Countries: Prospects for Cooperation," *Iranian Journal of International Affairs*, Vol.8, No.3, Fall 1996, pp.584-586.

President Saddam Hussein, probably more risk-taker than his predecessors, did not hesitate to invade two of his neighbors (Iran in 1980 and Kuwait in 1990). A main objective was to change the territorial configuration of Iraq at the expense of these two states. This policy created a legacy of distrust between the Iraqi leader and other Gulf-states rulers. It is hard to visualize any "normal" relations between Iraq on one side and other Gulf states such as Kuwait and Saudi Arabia on the other side as long as Saddam Hussein is in power. Put differently, a stable security system in the Persian Gulf is unlikely until Saddam leaves the scene. Thus, since the Gulf War all the seven Gulf states have supported the United Nations resolutions and sanctions against Iraq.

However, the severity of the sanctions and the publicity of the plight of the Iraqi people prompted some leaders in the Gulf and elsewhere to express sympathy toward the Iraqi people and to call for lifting of the sanctions. In 1990 no body expected the sanctions to last as long as they have. They have not weakened Saddam Hussein's grasp on power, meanwhile the sanctions have had devastating impact on the Iraqi people.[281] This made some people wonder how fair it is to punish an innocent population for the crimes of a dictator over whom they have no control.[282] In response to this misery of the Iraqi people, the Gulf monarchies confirmed their position that "The leaders were unanimous that the only way to end the suffering of the fraternal Iraqi people is for Iraq to implement all clauses of the Security Council resolutions in full.[283]"

Putting this unanimity aside, it is important to point out that some Gulf leaders have openly expressed their support of the rehabilitation and empowerment of Iraq. The strongest advocate of this policy is Sheikh Zayed Al Nahyan, president of the UAE, the country with the most serious problems

---

[281] According to one observer, "Concern has grown across the Arab world that the trade embargo on Iraq has done little to weaken its government and much to impoverish its people." See Rosemary Hollis, "Lessons for next Time," *The World Today*, Vol.54, No.4, April 1998, p.91.

[282] Eric Rouleau, "America's Unyielding Policy toward Iraq," *Foreign Affairs,* Vol.74, No.1, January/February 1995, p.69.

[283] This statement was issued at the end of the annual summit of the Gulf Cooperation Council (GCC) states, held in Kuwait in December 1997. See Faris Glubb, "Important Steps Forward," *Middle East International*, No.566, January 16, 1998, p.16.

with Iran. According to this argument, without strong Iraq there would be no counterweight to Iran. The current demilitarization of Iraq endangers regional stability because it produces imbalance of power in favor of Tehran.[284] Qatar, which is concerned about the "Saudi hegemony" over the six Gulf monarchies, has adopted similar stand. In this regard, it is important to recall that Baghdad's military arsenal was significantly depleted during the Gulf War and since then the country has had no major arms imports. In other words, even after reaching a political settlement with Iraq it will take some time to create a genuine balance of power between the three major Gulf states-Iran, Iraq, and Saudi Arabia.

Given the great concentration of power at the hands of President Saddam Hussein, it is very hard to make any credible prediction of what might happen in Iraq in the next several decades. Still two observations can be made. First, regardless of the Iraqi leader's presence or absence on the political scene it is highly unlikely that Baghdad will be satisfied with its territorial configuration. In other words, the Iraqi attempt to challenge and change the status quo is likely to endure well into the new millennium. It might take different form than a full-scale war. Instead, other forms of warfare such as terrorism and intimidation might prove more successful. Second, in spite of the statements of sympathy by some Gulf leaders and the genuine desire to create some form of balance of power in the region, it is unlikely that serious efforts will be made to get Saddam Hussein "out of the box." The current situation (i.e. a weakened and isolated Saddam in power under heavy international scrutiny) serves two purposes. It makes Gulf states less worry about potential threat from Iraq and it enhances their chances to maximize their oil revenues by keeping some of the Iraqi oil out of the international market (since 1990 there have been different restrictions on the amount of oil Baghdad is allowed to sell). Finally, it is important to point out that a change in the proliferation of weapons of mass destruction is likely to alter the security environment in the Persian Gulf region.

---

[284] Volker Perthes, Iraq Under Sanctions: A Regime Defiant, A Briefing Paper, The Royal Institute of International Affairs, No.40, February 1998, p.4.

WEAPONS OF MASS DESTRUCTION (WMD)

Over the last two decades there have been several military operations in the Persian Gulf states where weapons of mass destruction (chemical, biological, nuclear weapons and the missiles which carry them) were involved. One of the earliest developments was the Israeli pre-emptive strike against Osirak, the Iraqi nuclear reactor in June 1981. During the Iran-Iraq war missiles were used by the two sides in what became known as "the war of cities[285]," and Baghdad used chemical weapons against the Iranians and against its own Kurdish population. The most stunning development has been the continuous efforts by the international community to destroy the Iraqi stockpile of these non-conventional weapons since the Gulf War.

Baghdad's efforts to acquire and develop WMD go back to the mid 1970s. In cooperation with France and Italy, Iraq was able to construct an infrastructure for nuclear program.[286] The Israeli attack destroyed the reactor but did not end the Iraqi ambitious plan to stockpile all kinds of non-conventional weapons. During it's long war with Iran (1980-88) Baghdad took advantage of the Iranian rhetoric by presenting itself as a secular bulwark against the messianic Islamism coming out of Tehran. Accordingly, Iraq faced few restrictions in her efforts to accumulate all kinds of weapons. In addition, Baghdad's use of chemical weapons against the Iranians and the Kurds was met by little condemnation from the United States and other Western countries. However, the continuing build-up of Iraqi arsenal of these weapons paved the way for the show-down since the Gulf War.

At the end of the war, the United Nations Security Council passed resolution 687 (April 1991) which requested that Iraq agree to the destruction of all its WMD and allow United Nations supervised inspection of weapons sites. Accordingly, the United Nations Special Commission (UNSCOM) was

---

[285] In the 1980s Iraq had extensive ballistic missile capabilities including a stockpile of Soviet-supplied Scud-Bs and two indigenously-produced variants of the Scud-B, the Al-Husayn and the Al-Abbas. See U.S. Congress, Office of Technology Assessment, Technologies *Underlying Weapons of Mass Destruction*, Washington D.C.: U.S. Government Printing Office, December 1993, pp.209, 220-221.

[286] Ahmed Hashim, "Iraq: Profile of a Nuclear Addict," *The Brown Journal of World Affairs*, Vol.4, No.1, Winter/Spring 1997, p.106.

created. David Kay, the chief inspector of the three early UN nuclear weapons inspections stated that at the time of the Gulf War "Iraq was probably only 18 to 24 months away from its first crude nuclear device and no more than three to four years from more advanced, deliverable weapons.[287]" Put differently, the world was shocked how close Iraq came from having a nuclear device. It is worth mentioning that UNSCOM has done magnificent job in destroying the Iraqi stockpile of these weapons. In 1998 Kofi Annan, United Nations Secretary General, confirmed that the UNSCOM had succeeded in destroying more weapons in Iraq than were destroyed during the entire Gulf War.[288]

Thus, according to a UNSCOM report issued in early 1998 Iraq's ballistic missiles have been largely eliminated.[289] Furthermore, the report states, "Considerable quantities of chemical weapons, their components, and chemical weapons-related equipment have been destroyed.[290]" In another report the International Atomic Energy Agency (IAEA) said, "Iraq had successfully compiled a full, final and complete account of its past nuclear weapons programs.[291]" Still, much less progress has been achieved in locating and eliminating Iraq's biological weapons capability. Because of the dual-use character of many biological agents, verifying the presence of a biological warfare capability is inherently more difficult than monitoring nuclear or ballistic missile programs.

This stunning success raises the question of Baghdad's policy in regard to WMD in the future. In trying to predict the orientation of the current or future government in Baghdad toward non-conventional weapons two points should be taken into consideration. First, regardless of UNSCOM's efforts to destroy Iraq's stockpile, the "know-how" can not be eliminated.[292] The Iraqi scientists know how to assemble and manufacture these weapons. This knowledge

---

[287] David A. Kay, "Denial and Deception Practices of WMD Proliferators: Iraq and Beyond," *The Washington Quarterly*, Vol.18, No.1, Winter 1994, p.85.

[288] Christopher S. Wren, "Top UN. Arms Monitor is said to call Iraqi plans to end crisis inadequate," New York Times, February 6, 1998, p.A10.

[289] George A. Lopez and David Cortright, "Trouble in the Gulf: Pain and Promise," *The Bulletin of the Atomic Scientists*, Vol.54, No.3, May/June 1998, p.40.

[290] Ibid., p.41.

[291] Barbara Crossette, "A Clean Bill for the Iraqis on A-Arms? Experts Upset," New York Times, April 19, 1998, p.4.

[292] For a similar conclusion see David A. Kay, "Iraq Beyond the Crisis du Jour," *The Washington Quarterly*, Vol.21, No.3, Summer 1998, p.11.

cannot be taken away from them.[293] Second, the reasons for Iraqi heavy investment in acquiring and developing these weapons are still there and are not likely to change any time soon. The Iraqi leaders perceive their country in technological disadvantage with Israel and demographic disadvantage with Iran. The way to "correct" this imbalance, it has been proposed, is to develop chemical, biological, and nuclear capabilities. Thus, a long-term and lasting solution to the WMD in Iraq does not seem in sight in the near future. Meanwhile, no doubt, the Iraqis will keep watching the developments in Iran.

Iranian nuclear ambitions are, to a large extent, a reactionary replica of the Iraqi nuclear program.[294] Like others in the region and the rest of the world, Iran seems to have been completely surprised to discover how close Iraq had come to obtaining nuclear weapons.[295] Thus, if Iran is to be persuaded not to go nuclear, it must be convinced that an Iraqi nuclear program will not re-emerge sometime in the future. As has been discussed above, such assurances are hard to make.[296] As George Shultz, former US secretary of state put it, "proliferation begets proliferation[297]," in other words, as long as Iraq or Iran is pursuing nuclear capability, the other would follow suit.

Another explanation for Iran's nuclear ambitions is Israel. Since the Shah was overthrown in 1979 Jerusalem and Tehran have been strong enemies to each other. Israel is believed by most observers and intelligence agencies to be a nuclear power. As had been illustrated in the Israeli attack against the Iraqi reactor in 1981, Jerusalem would not hesitate to use all means, including the military ones, to prevent the emergence of another nuclear power in the

---

[293] A former inspector for the UNSCOM proposed that Western countries find a way to get Iraqi scientists and their families out of the country. See David Albright, "Masters of Deception," *The Bulletin of the Atomic Scientists*, Vol.54, No.3, May/June 1998, pp.44-50.

[294] Avner Cohen, "The Nuclear Issue in the Middle East in a New World Order," *Contemporary Security Policy*, Vol.16, No.1, April 1995, p.53.

[295] Shai Feldman, "Middle East Nuclear Stability: The State of the Region and the State of the Debate," *Journal of International Affairs*, Vol.49, No.1, Summer 1995, p.208.

[296] As an illustration of this reactionary policy and the connection between Iraq and the development of nuclear capability in Iran, in 1984-in the midst of the Iran-Iraq war-a new nuclear research center was opened in Asfahan, Iran.

[297] George Shultz, "Preventing the Proliferation of Nuclear Weapons," *Department of State Bulletin*, Vol.84, No.2093, December 1984, p.18.

Middle East. The Iranians seriously believe that Israel would attack their nuclear facilities. Developments in the late 1990s raise the stakes in this growing hostility between the Jewish state and the Islamic Republic. According to some reports Israel has been cultivating secret intelligence contacts with the Taliban, the Islamic movement in Afghanistan and a rival to Iran, with a view to installing sophisticated spying equipment to monitor Iranian nuclear arms development.[298] In addition, in 1998 Israel's capabilities of launching a pre-emptive attack on Iran's nuclear infrastructure were enhanced by the incorporation in Jerusalem's airforce of new F151 long-range strike aircraft.[299] Finally, Israel gained a second-strike nuclear option by adding to its navy three Dolphin class diesel-electric submarines which are considered among the most advanced in the world.[300] These submarines could fire cruise missiles from the sea.

In spite of these perceived threats from Iraq and Israel, the Iranian declared policy is that it neither seeks nor needs nuclear weapons. For example, shortly after he came to office Kamal Kharrazi, Iran's Foreign Minister, stated that "We are certainly not developing an atomic bomb, because we do not believe in nuclear weapon and its utility. We believe in and promote the idea of the Middle East as a region free from nuclear weapons and other weapons of mass destruction.[301]" Instead, the Iranians explain their interest in nuclear technology based on the need to alleviate the country's serious shortage of electrical generating capacity and to utilize it in medicine and agriculture. Furthermore, the argument goes, unlike India, Pakistan and Israel, Iran is a party to the Non-proliferation Treaty (NPT) and has pledged to cooperate with the (IAEA).[302] Finally, as an indication of Tehran's peaceful

---

[298] Christopher Walker, "Israel Pursues Afghan Ties to Spy on Tehran," Times on line, June 18, 1998.

[299] The $2.5 billion order for 25 of the world's most advanced fighters, plus spare parts, is due to be completed by the end of 1998. See Christopher Walker, "New Jets Enable Israelis to Hit Iran," The Times on line, June 25, 1998.

[300] British Broadcasting Corporation (BBC) World News on line, "Israel Buys New Subs," July 3, 1998.

[301] *Middle East Insight*, "An Exclusive Interview with Iran's Foreign Minister Dr. Kamal Kharrazi," Vol.13, No.1, November/December 1997, p.36.

[302] Iran's nuclear facilities will be the first test of the IAEA inspection program known as 93+2 (using powerful isotopic detection techniques), which was formulated after the agency discovered that Iraq had managed to systematically deceive

intention, Iran ratified the global treaty banning chemical weapons in late 1997.[303]

On the other side, critics of Iran's policy argue that the country is already rich in gas and oil resources and is seeking nuclear technology for military motives. They also point to Tehran ambitious program to strengthen its long-range missile capabilities. Iran is believed to have acquired technology from North Korea for the Scud-derivative Nodong surface-to-surface missile and to develop the C-801 cruise missile.[304]

Regardless of Iran's intentions and whether it has or does not have access to non-conventional weapons, the possibility of developing such weapons are there. Simply stated, Iran is vulnerable to Israel's nuclear capabilities and to Iraq's potential ones. Furthermore, Tehran does not have an allied superpower to rely on in the case of an attack by either of these two states. Unlike countries such as Saudi Arabia or Kuwait, Iran has to depend on itself.

CONCLUSION

At the brink of the new millennium the Persian Gulf seems to lack the ingredient of a long-term and lasting peace. The unsettled border disputes, the uncertainty about the future of Iraq and the unpredictability of non-conventional weapons all can be seen as "time bombs" threatening the stability of the region. The current Arab/Iranian rapprochement still is in its infant stage and it is hard to predict how far it will go. The soaring defense spending should be considered as a symptom for this high wall of mistrust between the eight Gulf states.

However, the future does not look completely bleak. Slowly and incrementally the region is becoming more integrated in the international system. Most of the Gulf states have already joined the International Trade Organization (ITO) or their applications are under consideration. Foreign investment is invited and welcomed in a growing number of states and in

---

IAEA inspectors. See *Middle East Monitor*, "Iran's Atomic Project Remains A Puzzle for Scientists," Vol.27, No.7, July 1997, p.53.

[303] *Middle East Economic Digest*, Vol.41, No.46, November 14, 1997, p.24.

[304] The International Institute for Strategic Studies, *The Military Balance*, New York: Oxford University Press, 1997, p.119.

broader economic sectors. In short, all over the region there is more interest in raising standards of living and improving economic conditions.

The plunge in oil prices in 1998 incited Gulf states to coordinate their economic policies. Stable oil prices is in their best interest. In other words, mutual economic interests can serve as a glue to consolidate regional cooperation. Bluntly, economic interests can pave the way for regional integration. In the near future there is no guarantee that the Gulf states will be able to overcome the differences between them. But in the long-run there are signs of hope and pragmatic considerations for a stable security environment. It won't be easy but a stable security system in the Gulf deserves the efforts.

Chapter 9

GLOBAL POWERS IN THE PERSIAN GULF: THE UNITED STATES, EUROPE, RUSSIA, AND CHINA

For hundreds of years foreign powers have shown strong interest in the Persian Gulf. It is not an exaggeration to state that external involvement has had an immense impact on shaping the socio-economic and political systems in the region. It is important to point out that the Portuguese, Dutch, and British were originally interested in the strategic location of the Gulf states on the main trade road between Europe and the East. The discovery of oil in the twentieth century drastically switched the focus from geo-politics to geo-economics. The Persian Gulf's tremendous energy resources are at the heart of foreign interest and involvement in the region. By far, oil is the most important commodity exchanged between the eight Gulf states and the rest of the world.

Since its discovery, oil has become a strategic commodity. World economy runs on oil (particularly the transportation sector) and there is no substitute in the foreseeable future. Thus, oil proved essential in the prosecuting of World War II and the economic recovery in its aftermath. In the closing years of the twentieth century, oil still is as important as it has always been. Given the huge reserves in the Persian Gulf and the projected deepened world-dependence on oil supplies from the region, it is apparent that access to the Gulf's oil is critical to the national interest of individual global powers and to the international economic prosperity. In other words, the non-interruption of oil supplies from the Persian Gulf at reasonable prices is critical to the global economic system. Given the high level of integration between world economies, all countries (importers and exporters) will suffer from any threat to the security of the Gulf states. In this context the Gulf War (in which more than thirty countries participated) can be seen as an embodiment of this perception of common threat and the need for mutual action.

For the last few decades there have been growing allegations of proliferation of weapons of mass destruction in the region. Several Gulf states are believed to have sought to acquire access to nuclear, chemical, biological weapons and long-range missiles. The proliferation of these non-conventional weapons poses additional threats to the stability of the region. Furthermore, since the early 1990s the change in the international system has altered the dynamics of the security environment. The bipolar system, which dominated the world for most of the second half of the twentieth century, has been replaced by a pluralistic one (more in the economic sphere and less in the military one). Thus, in the beginning of the new millennium four global powers (in addition to smaller ones) compete for oil and political influence in the Persian Gulf. These are the United States, Europe, Russia, and China. Each has its own economic and strategic agenda. Their policies have not always been in harmony and are likely to continue to contradict each other. Japan, another significant global power, has vast economic interest in the region. But, for a variety of reasons, Tokyo lacks political clout. Put differently, Japan has adopted a "business-like" approach to the Gulf region with very little, if any, interest in pursuing a military and political agenda.

In the next four sections the policies of the United States, Europe, Russia, and China in the Persian Gulf will be examined. The focus will be on two dimensions: oil-dependence and security. The analysis seeks to highlight the lack of common strategy between these players toward the region. These, sometimes, contradictory objectives and policies feed and contribute to instability in the region. It is the contention of this study that building a consensus based on common energy objectives would be in the best interest of the eight Gulf states, the four global powers, and world-wide economic prosperity.

THE UNITED STATES

The United States policy in the Persian Gulf is governed by oil. For several decades Washington has considered the non-interruption of oil supplies from the region a matter of national security. The growing American dependence on imported oil enforces this sense of vulnerability. For example in 1987 Washington imported 36.9 percent of its oil consumption.[305]. Ten years later, the figure jumped to 49.3 percent.[306] Equally important, the Department of Energy projects that by the year 2020 the United States will import 65.2 percent of its oil needs.[307] Transportation is at the center of the US oil dependence problem because it is by far the dominant consumer of petroleum products, accounting for two-thirds of oil use.[308] Furthermore, its demand for oil is highly inelastic. Unlike other industrialized countries, the tax system in the United States does not provide incentives to curb consumption. Among the member states of the Organization of Economic Cooperation and Development (OECD) Americans are the least-taxed users of gasoline.[309] In short, Washington's consumption of oil is on the rise and growing proportion will be imported from overseas.

The American vulnerability to the interruption of oil supplies has been clearly demonstrated in the 1970s. The so-called oil shocks (1973-74 and 1979) had tremendous negative impact on the overall economic performance

---

[305]The British Petroleum Company, *BP Statistical Review of World Energy*, London: The British Petroleum Company, 1998, pp. 10 & 18.

[306] Ibid.

[307] US Department of Energy, Energy Information Administration, *International Energy Outlook*, Washington DC: US Government Printing Office, 1998, pp.136 & 179.

[308] David L. Greene, "The Outlook for US Oil Dependence," *Energy Policy*, Vol.26, No.1, January 1998, p.61.

[309] Edward R. Fried and Philip H. Trezise, *Oil Security: Retrospect and Prospect*, Washington DC: The Brookings Institution, 1993, p.84.

including an increase in the unemployment rate and a decrease of the gross national product (GNP) growth rate.[310] Not surprisingly, in the last several decades Washington has shown growing interest and involvement in securing oil supplies from a leading source of energy-the Persian Gulf.

The strong US involvement in the Persian Gulf can be divided into three intertwined phases. The first one started shortly after World War II when Truman administration insisted on Soviet withdrawal from Iran.[311] It is important to point out that by that time the Iranian oil infrastructure was well-developed and well-integrated in the global market. The war demonstrated the significance of oil fields in Iran and the newly discovered ones in the other Gulf states. For the following several decades Washington enjoyed close and warm relations with the Pahlavi regime in Tehran. An illustration of this relations came early in 1950s when the Central Intelligence Agency (CIA) played a crucial role in what is known as "Ajax Operation" by which the Shah was re-instated at the helm in Tehran. This was followed by increasing the share of American companies in developing and exporting the Iranian hydrocarbon resources.

In addition to the close cooperation with the Shah of Iran, Washington has had very warm relations with the conservative Arab monarchies particularly Saudi Arabia. Thus, the United States played a leading role in containing the tide of Arab nationalism, then led by the Egyptian President Nasser. This was demonstrated during the Yemen crisis when military confrontations between Egypt and Saudi Arabia occurred and Washington's engagement resulted in the eventual withdrawal of the Egyptian forces from Yemen.

The second phase of the American involvement in the Persian Gulf was marked by the official British withdrawal from the region in 1971. This paved the way for US to fill the political vacuum and take the lead in creating a

---

[310] Several studies support this conclusion. For example see K. Mork, O. Olsen, and H. Mysen, "Macroeconomic Responses to Oil Price Increases and Decreases in Seven OECD Countries," *The Energy Journal*, Vol.15, No.4, December 1994, pp.19-35.

[311] For more details on this crisis and American involvement in the Middle East in general see George Lenczowski, *American Presidents and the Middle East*, Durham: Duke University Press, 1990.

security system in the region. In response to the bitter experience in Vietnam, Washington decided not to send American troops to defend the Gulf states. Instead, according to Nixon Doctrine[312] a twin-pillar strategy was adopted. Accordingly, Iran and Saudi Arabia took the direct responsibility of defending the region from any threat from hostile powers. The Iranian revolution in 1979 ended Tehran's participation in this strategy. This coincided with the Soviet invasion of Afghanistan which brought Moscow closer to the Gulf energy resources. The American response to these developments was documented in Carter Doctrine which declared that any threat to the Persian Gulf region would be regarded as an assault on vital interests of the US and will be repelled by any means necessary including military force.

The Soviet withdrawal from Afghanistan in the late 1980s reduced the direct external threat to the region. In addition the Iran-Iraq war (1980-88) kept the two regional powers busy fighting each other. Officially, US adopted a neutral position watching closely any change in the course of the war without direct intervention. However, at the end of the war (1987-88) and at the urging of the Kuwaiti government, the United States Joint Task Force escorted reflagged Kuwaiti oil tankers and several confrontations occurred between the American and Iranian navies. This active military presence in the Gulf paved the way for the third phase of American involvement in the region which started with the Iraqi invasion of Kuwait and still is in place.

Instead of defending oil resources from "over the horizon," the Gulf war resulted in a significant presence of US air and naval forces and the infrastructure for quick insertion of ground forces. Moreover, Several defense agreements were signed between Washington and the Gulf monarchies. In short, since 1990 the United States has resumed direct responsibility for the defense of oil shipments from the Persian Gulf. This active and direct security role is part of a broader political design aims at containing the military power of both Iran and Iraq and maintaining close cooperation with the six Gulf monarchies. The strong interest in the security of the region can be explained by its share in Washington total oil import as the following table shows.

---

[312] Nixon Doctrine stated that the US would no longer participate in local conflicts, but would provide the countries involved with military assistance.

Table I
United States Oil Imports in million (b/d), 1990-1997

Year	Total	Imports from the Gulf	Share in total
1990	7,161	1,961	27.3%
1991	6,626	1,835	27.6%
1992	6,938	1,774	25.5%
1993	7,618	1,775	23.3%
1994	8,054	1,722	21.3%
1995	7,886	1,563	19.8%
1996	8,498	1,594	18.7%
1997	9,158	1,747	19.0%

Source: United States Department of Energy, Energy Information Administration, *International Petroleum Statistics Report*, Washington DC: US Government Printing Office, 1998, p.49.

It is important to point out that since 1990 the US has imported very little oil from Iran and Iraq. Most of the oil came from the six Gulf monarchies. Indeed, Saudi Arabia provided most of it. Also, the declining share of the Gulf oil into the total American import should not be seen as a sign of "energy security" for two reasons. First, the American economy is part of an integrated and inter-dependent international economic system. Even if the United States imported not one drop of oil from the Gulf, a disruption of oil supplies from the region to European, Japanese, and Asian markets would have a negative impact on US export earnings, prices, and overall production and employment levels.[313] Second, in the long-term, the American economy is projected to grow more dependent on imported oil. United States' share of world proven reserves is only 2.9 percent while that of the Persian Gulf is 65.2 percent.[314]

These strong energy interests both at present and in the future explain Washington's heavy commitment to the defense of the region. At the same time, the petro-dollars have been used to finance one of the most ambitious

---

[313] William C. Ramsay, "Oil in the 1990s: The Gulf Dominant," p.56, in Phebe Marr and William Lewis, (eds.), Boulder, CO: Westview Press, 1993.

[314] British Petroleum Company, *BP Statistical Review of World Energy*, London: The British Petroleum Company, 1998, p.4.

armament plans in the world. The following table sheds lights on the circulation of these petro-dollars between the United States and the Gulf monarchies.

Table II
United States Exports of Major Conventional Weapons to the Gulf Monarchies
(1990-1997) at Constant 1990 prices

Country	1990	1991	1992	1993	1994	1995	1996	1997
Bahrain	392	51	29			38	210	13
Kuwait	5	54	947	646	25	456	1047	271
Oman	35		2	1	3	7	41	1
Qatar								
S. Arabia	1018	360	771	2187	1232	1048	1505	1692
UAE	23			101	234	20	171	
Total	1473	465	1749	2935	1494	1569	2974	1977

Source: Stockholm International Peace Research Institute (SIPRI), SIPRI Arms Transfer and Arms Production Projects, Stockholm: SIPRI, 1998, pp.1-4.

The figures show that from 1990 to 1997 the six Gulf monarchies imported weapons worth $14,636 billion from the United States. According to many security analysts this huge military expenditure has two major flaws. First, it highlights the ruling regimes' heavy dependence on foreign power to provide them with security. This has been a source of embarrassment and raised questions about the legitimacy of some of the royal families. It is worth mentioning that American troops in Saudi Arabia had already been the subject of two attacks which points to a degree of domestic resentment. Second, in case of internal turmoil there is very little American troops can do. Instead, these troops can only prevent the re-play of the Gulf War, (i.e. a cross-border aggression by one Gulf state against another one). In short, the strong American commitment to the security of the Gulf monarchies should not be taken as a guarantee for regional stability. This will be determined by how successful Washington's policy toward the other two Gulf states-Iraq and Iran.

Probably it is not an exaggeration to state that Washington had never had "warm" relations with Baghdad. In 1932 Iraq became an independent state and joined the League of Nations but the British influence dominated the country until the overthrow of the monarch in a bloody coup in July 1958. Shortly after the declaration of the republic Iraq withdrew from Baghdad Pact which included other pro-Western powers such as Iran, Turkey, Pakistan, and Britain. Another indicator of the continuous tension between Iraq and the United States is the fact that since 1958 the two countries had diplomatic relation for only 13 years, from 1958 to 1967 and from 1984 to 1990.[315]

During these years, the 1980s represent the best time between Washington and Baghdad. This can be explained by the presence of a common enemy-the Islamic regime in Tehran. Thus, regardless of Saddam Hussein's brutality, he was perceived as the only leader standing between Khomeini and the rest of the Middle East.[316] Accordingly, Iraq received generous financial support from the pro-Western Gulf monarchies and intelligence information from the United States. Saddam Hussein's use of chemical weapons against the Kurds and the Iranians was met with little, if any, condemnation from Washington. This "tolerance" of the Iraqi regime's practices was embodied in Reagan administration's decision to remove Iraq from the Department of State's list of states sponsoring international terrorism in 1982 which paved the way for the resumption of diplomatic relations between the two countries two years later.

The end of the Iran-Iraq war in favor of the latter removed the common objective Baghdad and Washington shared (eliminating the Iranian threat) and the decade of miscalculation came to an end with the Iraqi invasion of Kuwait in August 1990.[317] At the end of the Gulf War the universal conviction in Washington was that no political leader could survive the catastrophe that had been inflicted on Saddam Hussein.[318] But, against all the odds, he did. The question of what to do with Saddam Hussein was left to the Clinton administration. In a clear departure of traditional American policy, the Clinton administration rejected the strategy of exploiting the rivalry between Iran and

---

[315] For a detailed discussion of the American/Iraqi relations see Gawdat Bahgat, "Beyond Sanctions: US Policy Toward Iraq," *International Relations*, Vol.13, No.4, April 1997, pp.57-68.

[316] Zachary Karabell, "Backfire: US Policy Toward Iraq, 1988-2 August 1990," *Middle East Journal*, Vol.49, No.1, Winter 1995, p.30.

[317] Paul A. Gigot, "A Great American Screw-Up: The US and Iraq, 1980-1990," *National Interest*, No.22, Winter 1990/91, pp.3-10.

[318] Michael Sterner, "Closing the Gate: The Persian Gulf War Revisited," *Current History*, Vol.96, No.606, June 1997, p.19.

Iraq in favor of confronting both of them simultaneously.[319] For Iraq, this meant maintaining economic, diplomatic, and military pressure until Saddam Hussein is out of power.

In most of the 1990s, the American objective has been clear and constant: a unified Iraq at peace with its neighbors. At least three perceptions have shaped Washington's approach toward Baghdad and are likely to continue to have an impact in the foreseeable future. First, the nature of the political system in Baghdad. There is almost universal consensus in the American political establishment that normality in the relations with Iraq and stability in the Persian Gulf will not be restored as long as Saddam Hussein is in power. Furthermore, there is a growing realization and acknowledgement that there is no "democratic" Iraqi opposition movement. Put differently, the successor regime, when it comes, is likely to be similar to current one, albeit, less aggressive and less adventurous. Second, the longer the standstill with Iraq endures, the stronger the opposition to the sanctions policy both in US and abroad. In other words, it is hard to sustain support to the American stand against Iraq as memories of the Gulf War fade. For the last few years France, Russia, China, and other Arab countries have advocated reaching a compromise with the regime in Baghdad. Increasingly, Washington and London have been isolated in their determination to contain Saddam Hussein. Third, the means available to the United States to change the political environment in Iraq are limited. An American direct attack using ground forces is not an option. Air strikes hurt but have no chance of changing the political system. Assassination is prohibited by a series of presidential executive orders.

Given these restrictions (nature of Iraqi opposition groups, the problem of maintaining domestic[320] and international support, and the available methods to change the political system in Baghdad), American efforts to remove

---

[319] Michael C. Hudson, "To Play the Hegemon: Fifty Years of US Policy toward the Middle East," *Middle East Journal*, Vol.50, No.3, Summer 1996, p.340.

[320] As an example of domestic opposition, an American group of more than 90 people went to Iraq in May 1998 to protest American backing of the sanctions by delivering about $4 million in medical aid to Baghdad. The delegation was led by Ramsey Clark, a former Attorney General in the Johnson Administration, and Thomas J. Gumbleton, a retired Roman Catholic bishop from Detroit. See Barbara Crossette, "UN Lifts Travel Ban on Iraqis Without Objection from US," New York Times, May 9, 1998, p.A5.

Saddam Hussein have not succeeded. For the foreseeable future, it is likely that Washington's approach toward Baghdad would focus on the following guidelines: To support the dismantling of Iraqi weapons of mass destruction, to keep working with different Iraqi opposition groups, to approve more humanitarian aid to the Iraqi people, and to promote the idea of opening a dialogue with future Iraqi government. It is unclear how far these guidelines can achieve. Rather, what is certain is that resuming economic and diplomatic relations between Washington and Baghdad is highly unlikely as long as Saddam Hussein is in power. The tension between the two countries is likely to endure. This pessimistic projection is, to some degree, reversed with regard to the other Persian Gulf power-Iran.

The Islamic revolution in 1979 put an end to the very close relations the United States had with Iran under the Pahlavi regime for more than three decades. During the Iran-Iraq war Washington adopted a neutral stand but close to the end it tilted more toward Baghdad. In the early 1990s, there was an opportunity to improve relations between the two countries due to the "responsible" (i.e. neutral) position Iran took in the Gulf War. However, this opportunity was missed and in most of the 1990s there had been several setbacks. These included the executive order issued by President Clinton in May 1995 that prohibited all trade with and financial services to the Islamic Republic.[321] A year later, August 1996, the president signed into law the Iran-Libya Sanctions Act (ILSA), which imposed sanctions on foreign companies that made new investments worth more than $40 million (later the amount was reduced to $20 million) for the development of energy sector in Iran or Libya.[322]

The 1997 presidential elections in Iran provided a potential turning point in this deteriorated relations between Washington and Tehran and indeed, in the political direction the Islamic Republic might take in the future. The landslide victory of Muhammad Khatami, a moderate cleric, proved a degree of pluralism in the Iranian political system and strengthened the moderate

---

[321] For a discussion of this executive order see Gary Sick, "Rethinking Dual Containment," *Survival*, Vol.40, No.1, Spring 1998, pp.5-32.

[322] For an analysis of this act see Laurie Lande, "Second Thoughts," *The International Economy*, Vol.11, No.3, May/June 1997, pp.44-49.

faction within the ruling elites.[323] In less than a year after he resumed power, Khatami has shown strong determination to improve relations with the outside world including the United States.[324] President Clinton, Secretary Albright and other high officials in Washington stated that they are convinced that Iran under Khatami is not the same as it was before the 1997 elections.[325]

In this context, some of the issues which complicated the relations between the two countries in the last several years have been addressed and deserve special attention. These are terrorism, the Arab-Israeli peace process, weapons of mass destruction, and the so-called pipeline diplomacy.

For long time Washington has accused Tehran of sponsoring international terrorism against the dissidents of the Islamic regime and against American targets. A recent report published by the US Department of State stated, "Tehran continued to be involved in the planning and execution of terrorist acts by its own agents and by surrogates and continued to fund and train known terrorist groups.[326]" The Iranians deny these accusations. In addition, American intelligence officials said they have concluded that President Khatami is sincerely lobbying for an end to government support of terrorism and that its activities are continuing only because he has not yet consolidated his control over the relevant security and intelligence services.[327]

Since the beginning of the Palestinian-Israeli peace process in the aftermath of the Gulf War, Iran has been one of a handful of states which openly expressed its opposition. Making peace between the Palestinians and the Israelis has been a major goal for American Middle Eastern policy for a long time. Thus, Tehran's opposition to the peace process represents a direct challenge to one of the most fundamental objective of Washington in the

---

[323] For a discussion of Khatami's potential impact on the political system in Tehran see Mark N. Katz, "The Khatami Factor: How Much Does It Matter?" *The National Interest*, No.51, Spring 1998, pp.85-90.

[324] In early January 1998 President Khatami gave an interview to the Cable News Network (CNN) in which he called for a "dialogue between civilizations" (i.e. cultural exchange between Iran and the US).

[325] Thomas W. Lippman, "Iranian President to Visit UN," Washington Post, June 28, 1998, p.A25.

[326] United States Department of State, *Patterns of Global Terrorism*, Washington DC: US Government Printing Office, 1998, p.31.

[327] Jeffrey Smith, "Khatami Wants to End Terrorism, Officials Say," Washington Post, May 5, 1998, p.A9.

region. In the last several years high-ranking Iranian officials said that their opposition is a matter of principle and Tehran does not wish to intervene in practice and physically disrupt the process. More to the point, in December 1997 President Khatami told Palestinian leader Yasser Arafat that "Whatever the Palestinians can agree to with Israel we (the Iranians) can live with.[328]"

Tehran's efforts to acquire biological, chemical, and nuclear weapons as well as ballistic missiles are of great concern to Washington. Ironically, Iran's interest in developing a nuclear infrastructure goes back to 1957, when it signed an agreement with the United States to cooperate in the field of nuclear technology. In 1974, the Shah established the Atomic Energy Organization of Iran. Two years later, he signed a contract with Kraftwerk Union, a German company, to build two nuclear power plants in Bushehr. The Iranian interest in acquiring nuclear technology has been re-energized in the closing years and in the aftermath of its war with Iran. Tehran claims that it is interested in the peaceful use of nuclear energy. Washington alleges that Iran is seeking to develop nuclear weapons. In line with these allegations, Washington has not spared efforts to block any cooperation between the Islamic Republic and foreign countries in transferring nuclear technology. Under intense pressure from Washington, Brazil, France, and India decided to close down peaceful nuclear exports to Iran. Germany decided not to complete the two nuclear reactors in Bushehr. Russia and China have come under mounting pressure to end their cooperation with Tehran. In addition, if Iran does manage to achieve substantial progress in developing its nuclear infrastructure, pre-emptive or covert military operations by the United States or some of its allies (i.e. Israel) should not be ruled out.[329]

Finally, Russia's stranglehold over current pipeline arrangements in the Caspian Basin has been a source of dismay not only for the Caspian states, who desperately need hard currency revenues from the export of oil and gas to facilitate economic reform, but also for international investors, who seek unhindered access to world markets.[330] Thus, supplements to the Russian-dominated pipeline system have been sought since 1993. In commercial terms,

---

[328] *Middle East Economic Digest*, Vol.42, No.7, February 13, 1998, p.21.

[329] For more details see Gawdat Bahgat, "Beyond Containment: US-Iranian Relations at a Crossroads," *Security Dialogue*, Vol.28, No.4, December 1997, pp.458-459.

[330] Michael P. Croissant, "US Interests in the Caspian Sea Basin," *Comparative Strategy*, Vol.16, No.4, October/December 1997, p.356.

the preferred route is through Iran to the Indian Ocean. The Islamic Republic's existing network of oil and gas pipelines and related infrastructure provide the lowest-cost outlet for Caspian Basin production. Furthermore, unlike other potential routes, Iran's is not exposed to immediate disruption due to war or insurrection. Despite these advantages, the Clinton administration has been strongly opposed to pipelines which transit Iran.[331] Given the financial and strategic implications for the chosen routes, this issue is likely to be on the agenda of any potential dialogue between Washington and Tehran in the future.

To sum up, in the closing years of the twentieth century both the United States and the Islamic Republic have shown interest in reducing or freezing the tension between them. However, the wall of mistrust which had been built over the last two decades will not be turned down overnight. There will be several setbacks, but the potential of rapprochement does exist.

In conclusion, it seems that four characteristics are likely to dominate the United States policy in the Persian Gulf in the foreseeable future. First, the security of oil supplies from the region will continue to be a major American national interest. Meanwhile, the six Gulf monarchies are not projected to have the capability to defend themselves. Thus, most likely Washington will maintain its heavy military presence in the Gulf region. As one scholar put it, "America's interests in the Gulf were now thought to be too important to be left to the regional powers to manage.[332]" Second, there is no indication that the clerical regime in Tehran or the Saddam regime (or a similar one) in Baghdad will collapse any time soon. Thus, a long-term strategy to "rehabilitate" them might have a better chance of success than pure punishment. Put differently, a strategy combines a mix of incentives and penalties, stick and carrot, might enhance the chances for stability in the region. It is important to point out that American oil companies have been

---

[331] In May 1998 Secretary of State Madeline Albright said, "US will continue to encourage alternative routes for the transport of Caspian energy resources." See *Middle East Economic Survey*, Vol.26, No.23, June 8, 1998, p.32.

[332] Geoffrey Kemp, "The United States, Europe, and the Persian Gulf," p.106 in Robert D. Blackwill and Michael Sturmer, (eds.), *Allies Divided: Transatlantic Policies for the Greater Middle East*, Cambridge, MA: The MIT Press, 1997.

lobbying for a change in the sanctions policy.[333] Third, progress in the Palestinian-Israeli peace process will improve the American credibility in the region. There is strong connection between the two conflicts. Some people in the Gulf accuse Washington of being too soft on Israel and too harsh on Iraq. Moreover, the sluggish peace process has been a source of embarrassment to the leaders of the Gulf monarchies. In this context, the American-Israeli-Turkish joint maneuvers early in 1998 were seen with a great deal of skepticism in all the eight Gulf states.[334] Fourth, given Washington's military power and the leading role it took in the Gulf War, there is no doubt that the United States will always have a special role in the security of the Gulf. This "special" role should not be seen as an "exclusive" one. Stability in the Gulf will be enhanced by cooperation between the United States and other major global powers.

EUROPE

Three characteristics can explain European policy in the Persian Gulf.[335] First, unlike the United States, European powers have long historical ties with most of the Gulf states. Some of the Gulf sheikdoms and Iraq were directly controlled by Britain for a prolonged period of time. This historical background as well as the geographical approximation between the two regions have strengthened their cultural ties. Accordingly, London and Paris are the centers of several Gulf financial institutions and newspapers (both anti and pro Gulf regimes). Second, this close contact between the two sides has been enhanced by European position on the Arab-Israeli conflict. In Arab

---

[333] Several corporations created lobby to convince the Congress and the administration to lift or moderate American sanctions all over the world. For details see their web site: WWW.USAENGAGE.COM.

[334] In January 1998 naval vessels from Israel, Turkey and the United States extended their first joint maneuver into international waters off the coast of Israel. The exercise was called Reliant Mermaid.

[335] It is important to point out from the outset that there is no one coherent and unified European policy. Rather, each country has its own approach. Nevertheless, one can identify common aspects in the policies of Britain, France, Germany and other European countries which differentiate them from that of the United States.

eyes, Europe has adopted a "less bias stand" than that of the United States. This can be explained partly by the power of the Jewish lobby in Washington and partly by European economic and energy interests in the Persian Gulf in particular and the whole Middle East in general. Third, as the following table demonstrates, Europe is more dependent on oil supplies from the Persian Gulf than the United States.

Table III
Europe Oil Imports in Million (b/d), 1990-1997

Year	Total	Imports from the Gulf	Share of total
1990	8,210	3,908	47.6
1991	8,588	3,660	42.6
1992	8,459	3,666	43.3
1993	8,127	4,048	49.8
1994	7,355	3,506	47.6
1995	7,226	3,365	46.5
1996	7,339	3,171	43.2
1997	7,487	3,414	45.5

Source: United States Department of Energy, Energy Information Administration, *International Petroleum Statistics Report*, Washington DC: US Government Printing Office, 1998, p.51.

The figures show how critical oil supplies from the Persian Gulf are to Europe. Thus, given the historical/cultural ties, the political stand on the Arab-Israeli conflict, and the deep energy dependence, European countries have significant stake in promoting and preserving stability in the Persian Gulf. This, however, is restrained by the fact that Europe, both as individual states and as one unit, is not match to the United States when it comes to military power and security. Put differently, in comparison with Europe, Washington has the upper hand in drawing defense policy in the Persian Gulf. This can be illustrated by the following table.

The figures show that in spite of Europe's deep dependence on imported oil from the Persian Gulf, there is a huge gap between European involvement in the region's security system and that of the United States. Still, Europe has sought to advance its interests by consolidating its economic ties to the Gulf states. According to the International Monetary Fund (IMP) the volume of trade between Europe as one economic bloc, and some individual European states, and the eight Gulf states is larger than that between the latter and Washington.[336] Put differently, Europe, as a trade partner, is more important to the Gulf states than the United States. Furthermore, the Gulf Cooperation Council (GCC) and the European Union (EU) have been engaged in negotiations for a long time to promote economic cooperation between the two blocs.[337]

Table IV
Europe Exports of Major Conventional Weapons to
The Gulf States (1990-1997) at Constant 1990 Prices

Country	1990	1991	1992	1993	1994	1995	1996	1997
Bahrain					14		9	
Iran	22	22	10	10	10	20		
Iraq	302							
Kuwait	18	22				379	212	139
Oman	109		25	16	189	168	256	172
Qatar	12	12	44	15	14	15	349	286
S. Arabia	996	737	147	400	24	42	291	678
UAE	786	300	52	427	184	231	478	791
Total	2245	1093	278	868	435	855	1595	2066

Source: Stockholm International Peace Research Institute (SIPRI), *Arms Transfer and Arms Production Projects*, Stockholm: SIPRI, 1998, pp.1-4.

In addition to this close cooperation with the six Gulf monarchies, several European countries have had better relations with Baghdad than Washington. In an attempt to break his isolation and to get the United Nations sanctions lifted, President Saddam Hussein has tried to create divisions between the five members of the Security Council. Accordingly, Iraq has offered lucrative, long-term oil deals to Russia, China, and France to get them to push for the lifting of sanctions while giving them a stake in the survival of his political

---

[336] International Monetary Fund, *Direction of Trade Statistics Yearbook*, Washington DC: International Monetary Fund, 1996.

[337] Rosemary Hollis, "Europe and the Middle East: Power by Stealth?" *International Affairs*, Vol.73, No.1, January 1997, p.26.

system.[338] France, which had close relations with Iraq since the mid 1970s, has not wasted this opportunity to re-establish itself as Baghdad's closest Western ally. Thus, Paris showed more tolerance to the Iraqi military operation in the northern part of the country (late August 1996) than London and Washington. In 1997, the French Cultural Center in Baghdad was re-opened. Most important, in preparation for the post-sanctions Iraq, the French oil companies, particularly Total and Elf Aquitaine, have negotiated several deals with the Iraqi government. Other European companies include Agip of Italy and Repsol of Spain.[339] These negotiations of oil deals have been accompanied by visits by high ranking Iraqi officials to Paris. No wonder, for the last few years France has been in favor of lifting the economic sanctions.

Similarly, Paris has been in the front in advocating an accommodative approach in drawing a Western policy toward Iran. Like the United States, Europe has its own reservations on the Islamic Republic's political practices. But unlike Washington, Brussels has chosen engagement instead of containment. At the EU summit in Edinburgh in December 1992, critical dialogue became official European policy.[340] Its aim is to change the Iranian regime's behavior through extensive economic, political, and cultural interactions between the two sides. In other words, both the United States and Europe share similar reservations, indeed rejection, of some Iranian policies. They disagree on how to change them.

A good illustration of the differences between these two approaches came in September 1997 when the National Iranian Oil Company (NIOC) signed an agreement with Total of France, Gazprom of Russia, and Petronas of Malaysia to invest $2 billion to develop the South Pars oil field. The deal was clear defiance to the American policy as stated in the ILSA of 1996. French officials, supported by other Europeans, backed the agreement and viewed the American law as "Extra-territorial bullying.[341]" After months of negotiations

---

[338] Adekeye Adebajo, "Saddam's Bazaar," *The World Today*, Vol.54, No.3, March 1998, p.62.

[339] *Middle East Economic Digest*, "Oil firms vie for new deals," Vol.42, No.15, April 10, 1998, p.27.

[340] Johannes Reissner, "Europe, the United States, and the Persian Gulf," p.138, in Robert D. Blackwill and Michael Sturmer, (eds.), *Allies Divided: Transatlantic Policies for the Greater Middle East*, Cambridge, MA: MIT Press, 1997.

[341] Zbigniew Brzezinski, Brent Scowroft, and Richard Murphy, "Differentiated Containment," *Foreign Affairs*, Vol.76, No.3, May/June 1997, p.28.

between Brussels and Washington the Clinton administration decided in May 1998 to waive sanctions and not to oppose future European investments in Iran.[342] The agreement, therefore sets a precedent allowing non-US firms to help Iran develop oil fields in the future without fear of a retaliation from Washington.[343] Accordingly, several oil companies have signaled their interest in investing in Iran's energy resources including Agip of Italy, Elf Aquitaine of France. Equally important, the British Petroleum Company (BP), which began as the Anglo-Persian Oil Company in 1908 but lost its leading role in Iran after the 1979 revolution, decided to open a representative office in Tehran. It is important to point out that Tehran sees the oil investment deals as not only economically beneficial but a strategic security asset as well. In other words, the presence of these foreign oil companies with their huge capital in the Gulf can serve as a security guarantee.

In spite of this European interest in developing Iran's energy resources, it is important to discuss two impediments in the rapprochement between Tehran and Brussels: the Fatwa (edict) against the British writer Salman Rushdie and the so-called Mykonos trial.

In 1989 the late Supreme Leader Ayatollah Ruhollah Khomeini issued a binding opinion pronouncing a sentence of death on the British author Salman Rushdie for writing a novel, The Satanic Verses, the content of which was considered to be blasphemous. Immediately, the fatwa was condemned by the Ministers of Foreign Affairs of the members of the then European Community, and senior-level diplomatic contacts between Brussels and Tehran were suspended. A month later, the European ambassadors returned to Tehran. Meanwhile, after tremendous pressure, then, President Rafsanjani stated that the fatwa was a religious issue, not a political one, implying that the government cannot change it, and declared that no official state organ would carry out the sentence against Rushdie. In spite of this unresolved situation, economic ties have since continued to grow.

---

[342] The exception is any investment in constructing pipelines to export production from the Caspian Basin.

[343] *Oil and Gas Journal*, "US Waives Sanctions on South Pars Field," Vol.96, No.21, May 25, 1998, p.18.

In some ways, the Mykonos verdict resembles the Rushdie affair. In April 1997, a German court concluded that Iran's top religious and political leaders had been behind the assassination of four Kurdish dissidents in Berlin five years before. After a meeting of its foreign ministers in Luxembourg later in the month, the European Union's leaders adopted several measures to punish Iran including halting bilateral ministerial visits and denying visas to Iranians holding intelligence and security posts. Again, there was little impact on the extensive economic relations and the European ambassadors went back to Tehran in November 1997. Few months later, the ban on high-level contacts with Iran was lifted.[344]

In closing two conclusions can be drawn from this discussion of European policy in the Persian Gulf. First, it is apparent that Europe has an extensive economic, financial, and trade ties with the Gulf states. Given the fact that oil fields in the North Sea are projected to be depleted in the near future, Europe will grow more dependent on imported oil from the Gulf. Meanwhile, the Gulf states need and reliance on European technology are likely to persist. Thus, one can expect the close economic cooperation between Europe and the Gulf states to endure. This means that in the foreseeable future the Gulf region will continue to be the scene of a strong competition between European and American economic interests. In the military sphere, however, the United States will keep playing a dominant role with little competition from Europe. This leads to the second conclusion that is the Iranians and some Arabs would welcome, indeed encourage, a growing European presence in the region as a counterweight to the United States. This will be applied to other global powers-Russia and China.

RUSSIA

Russian policy in the Persian Gulf is a little bit more complicated than that of the United States and Europe. It reflects both the Soviet legacy and the historical ties between Moscow and the eight Gulf states. Traditionally, Iraq was the closest ally the Soviet Union had in the Persian Gulf during most of

---

[344] Gawdat Bahgat, "The New Iran: A Myth Or A Reality?" *Asian Affairs*, Vol.85, No.2, June 1998, p.149.

the Cold War years.[345] The Pahlavi regime and the conservative Gulf monarchies did not have much interaction with Moscow. The overthrow of the Shah in 1979 did not improve relations with Tehran. During the Iran-Iraq war (1980-88) the Soviet Union continued to be a major supplier of arms to Iraq. Soviet-made missiles were used extensively by Baghdad to attack Tehran and other Iranian targets. In the 1990s, the collapse of the Soviet Union and its replacement by Russia has had a drastic impact on Moscow's policy in the Gulf region. The most important characteristic of Russian policy in the region, as well as in the rest of the world, is that it is driven more by economic interests and less by ideology. Put differently, since the early 1990s geo-economic incentives have become more importance in determining Russian foreign policy.

This increasing concern in promoting Russian economic interests is reflected in signing oil deals with Iraq and selling weapons and nuclear technology to those who can and want to pay for them. Thus, in March 1997 a consortium of Russian firms comprising Lukoil, Zarubazhneft and Machinoimport signed an agreement with the Iraq National Oil Company (INOC) to develop the 15 billion barrel West Qurna oil field.[346] Moscow's interest in Baghdad's energy resources partly explains Russian support of lifting the economic sanctions against Iraq. In addition, Russia is concerned about Iraq's financial capability to pay back its $7 billion debt to Moscow.[347]

---

[345] As an embodiment of this cooperation Moscow and Baghdad signed a Treaty of Friendship in 1972.

[346] United States Department of Energy, Energy Information Administration, Country Report: Iraq, Washington DC: US Government Printing Office, February 1998, p.9.

[347] In order to ease Russian opposition to the sanctions some scholars called upon the United States to lead a group of investors to buy Russia's Iraq debt. See Adam Garfinkle, "Liening on Saddam," The Washington Quarterly, Vol.21, No.3, Summer 1998, p.16.

Table V
USSR/Russia Exports of Major Conventional Weapons to
The Gulf States (1990-97) at Constant 1990 Prices

Country	1990	1991	1992	1993	1994	1995	1996	1997
Bahrain								
Iran	586	501	176	462	43		182	
Iraq	447							
Kuwait					5	127	65	
Oman								
Qatar								
S. Arabia								
UAE			114	136	181	186	36	18
Total	1033	501	290	598	229	313	283	18

Source: Stockholm International Peace Research Institute (SIPRI), *SIPRI Arms Transfer and Arms Production Projects*, Stockholm: SIPRI, 1998, pp.1-4.

Besides this interest in taking share in Iraq's hydrocarbon resources, Moscow has sought to sell arms to the other Gulf states as the above table shows.

The figures show the limited success Russia has achieved in selling arms to the region particularly in comparison with the United States and Europe. Due to the United Nations sanctions, Iraq has not been allowed to import weapons since its invasion of Kuwait in 1990. The Gulf monarchies have been traditional customers of Western arms industry. Thus, Iran provided the main market for Russian weapons in the Gulf. This cooperation in armament between Tehran and Moscow has expanded to cover nuclear technology and missile-related equipment.

The Bushehr plant is one of the most important project in Iran's efforts to develop nuclear infrastructure. Work on this reactor began in 1974 by a German firm and by the outbreak of the revolution in 1979, 80 percent of the infrastructure was completed. Given the political chaos which accompanied the revolution and the damage caused by the war with Iraq, the work in Bushehr was halted. In January 1995, progress on the plant was resumed when

Russia signed a $780-million contract to complete the work.[348] The United States strongly opposes the project. For the last several years Washington has been trying to persuade Moscow to stop its nuclear cooperation with Tehran with no success. On the contrary, there have been some reports on plans to provide Iran with more nuclear reactors in the near future. Furthermore, Moscow is reported to have supplied Tehran with SS-4 missile-related equipment.[349] This Russian help to develop Iran's missile capabilities has been of great concern in the United States.

This close cooperation between Moscow and Tehran points out to their geo-political and strategic mutual interests.[350] In 1996, Ali Akbar Velayati, then Iran Foreign Minister, stated that "Iran-Russia relations have never been so good in the past 500 years.[351]" These warm relations between the two countries can be explained by the fact that both of them need each other. Russia, as has been the case with Europe, opposes Washington's efforts to isolate Iran and sees it as an important strategic ally in the vital Persian Gulf region. In addition, politically, close ties with Tehran serves the Yeltsin government to placate Russian nationalists by showing Moscow's independence from the West.[352] In other words, the resentment and resistance of some leaders in the Kremlin to the new unilateral world order with the United States on top have added more incentives for co-operation with other countries including China and Iran. On the other side, the attempt by the Islamic Republic to improve relations with Moscow, and other countries, can be seen, partly, as a response to the American sanctions. Most important the two countries have been driven by their mutual interest in Central Asia and the Caucasus.

---

[348] United States Department of Energy, Energy Information Administration, *Country Report: Iran*, Washington DC: US Government Printing Office, March 1998, p.22.

[349] The International Institute for Strategic Studies, *The Military Balance*, New York: Oxford University Press, 1997, p.118.

[350] For more details on the evolution of Russian/Iranian relations see Martin Sicker, *The Bear and the Lion*, New York: Praeger, 1988.

[351] Cited in Adam Tarock, "Iran and Russia in 'Strategic Alliance'," *Third World Quarterly*, Vol.18, No.2, 1997, p.208.

[352] *Middle East Monitor*, "Moscow Ignores German Ruling Moves To Strengthen Ties With Iran," Vol.27, No.4, April 1997, p.28.

Moscow and Tehran share at least three major objectives in Central Asia and the Caucasus. First, for Russia, promoting cooperation with Iran is an important factor in its efforts to contain the rise of Islamic assertiveness within its own borders. The civil war in Chechnia is a case-in-point. In general, Tehran gave very little help, if any, to the rebels preferring to maintain its strategic and economic ties with Moscow. Second, since the break-up of the Soviet Union, some leaders in Russia have shown interest in maintaining some form of hegemony over the former Soviet republics. Thus, with the exception of the 3 Baltic states and Azerbaijan, Russian troops are deployed in every one of these republics. However, some of these states are trying to achieve a real independence from Moscow by approaching Western powers. Turkey, a traditional regional power with strong historical and cultural ties with many of the Central Asian states, serves as a connection and a bridge between the region and the West. Both Russia and Iran resist Turkish, and Western, penetration and influence in the Central Asia and the Caucasus. Thus, in the conflict between Azerbaijan and Armenia, Moscow and Tehran support the latter while Ankara backs the former. Furthermore, Russia and Iran have been on the same side in other regional civil wars such as the one in Tajikistan and Afghanistan. The glue which brought them together is their resistance to Western (particularly American) influence in what they consider as their own "backyard" or what the Russians describe as the "near-abroad."

The third common goal between Moscow and Tehran is utilizing the immense hydrocarbon wealth in the Caspian Basin. During the Soviet era the Caspian was shared by the Soviet Union and Iran. The two countries signed two agreements to regulate the use of the Basin. The 1921 Treaty of Friendship provided equal navigational rights and the 1940 Treaty of Commerce and Navigation specified an exclusive fishing zone along the coast of each country.[353] Beyond these boundaries the two states shared rights in the rest of the basin. The break-up of the Soviet Union changed the political map of the region. Instead of only Iran and the Soviet Union, five counties (Russia, Iran, Azerbaijan, Turkmenistan, and Kazakhstan) share the Caspian. More important, the last three enjoy substantial oil and natural gas resources on their side of the Basin and the first two (Russia and Iran) have very little. This raised the question whether the Caspian is a sea or a lake. General principles

---

[353] Dilip Hiro, "Troubled Waters: The Legal Status of the Caspian Sea," *Middle East International*, No.574, May 8, 1998, p.19.

of international law provide that seas can be partitioned while lakes are treated as legal condominiums to be used by all littoral states. In the first half of the 1990s, Russia and Iran claimed that the 1921 and 1940 treaties were still valid, implying that all countries bordering the Caspian must approve any offshore oil and gas developments. However, in early 1998 Moscow made a crucial shift in its position. It agreed that the seabed and the mineral reserves beneath it could be divided into national sector, meanwhile, the sea waters would be managed jointly by all the five littoral states.[354] In line with this new attitude, Russia and Kazakhstan signed an agreement in July 1998 to divide up the northern part of the Caspian. Iran opposes this approach and declared that "any change in the legal status of the basin can be resolved only through the unanimous agreement of all the five states.[355]" It is apparent that a comprehensive treaty covering maritime security, navigation and the exploitation of sea water and sea-bed resources acceptable to the five littoral states is not in sight in the near future.

To sum up, in most of the 1990s Russian policy in the Persian Gulf has been driven more by economic incentives and less by ideology. This trend is likely to continue in the twenty-first century. The same projection applies to another global power-China.

CHINA

China's involvement in the Persian Gulf came much later than most of the other global powers. For most of the Cold War years, Chinese policy was driven by ideological considerations-Beijing's relationship with the two superpowers. Chairman Mao Zedong viewed the region as part of the battle between the superpowers for global hegemony and advocated that foreign powers be kept out of the whole Middle East.[356] The domestic changes in China and the focus on economic modernization since the late 1970s have had significant impact on Beijing's policy in the Persian Gulf. For the last two decades, the Chinese economy has been one of the fastest growing economy

---

[354] *The Economist*, "Caspian Carve-up," Vol.346, No.8058, March 7, 1998, p.66.

[355] BBC News on Line, "Iran Attacks Caspian Oil Deal," July 8, 1998.

[356] Jonathan Rynhold, "China's Cautious New Pragmatism in the Middle East," *Survival*, Vol.38, No.3, Fall 1996, p.102.

in the world. According to the World Bank, the average annual growth rate of China's gross national product (GNP) per capita from 1985 to 1995 was 8.3 percent, the highest in the world.[357] This sustained economic growth as well as the country's huge population (more than 1.2 billion people) have raised concern about the availability of oil resources to meet the soaring domestic needs.

The 1950s represented a turning point in oil exploration in China. Two major field complexes at Karamay and Daqing were discovered in 1955 and 1959 respectively. Together they hold 40 percent of the country's total production.[358] Accordingly, China achieved net exporter status in 1959.[359] However, the staggering economic expansion made the country a net oil importer since 1993.[360] This disparity between production and consumption is projected to increase in the twenty-first century as the following table demonstrates.

Table VI
Oil Consumption and Production in China (1995-2020)
In Million of Barrels Per Day (b/d)

	1995	2000	2005	2010	2015	2020
Consumption	3.3	4.4	5.6	7.0	8.8	11.2
Production	2.9	3.4	3.5	3.6	3.6	3.5

Source: United States Department of Energy, International Energy Outlook, Washington DC: US Government Printing Office, 1998, pp.136 & 179.

It is also important to point out that at the end of the twentieth century, China is the second largest oil consumer in the world trailing only the United

---

[357] *The World Bank, World Development Report*, New York: Oxford University Press, 1997, Table 1, p.214.

[358] C.J. Campbell, "As Depletion Increases, Energy Demand Rises," Petroleum Economist, Vol.64, No.9, September 1997, p.113.

[359] Alan Jones, Giovanella D'Andrea and German Rodriguez, "China: Energy Sector Growth Vital for Further Economic Development," *Petroleum Economist*, Vol.64, No.9, September 1997, p.72.

[360] Editorial, "China Preparing itself for the Next Century," *Petroleum Economist*, Vol.65, No.4, April 1998, p.19.

States.[361] Furthermore, given Beijing's limited proven reserves, the country will grow more dependent on imported oil. Thus, the widening gap between consumption and production will be filled by oil supplies from the Persian Gulf and the Caspian Basin. Accordingly, in late 1997 China signed a major oil deal with Kazakhstan worth an estimated $9.5 billion, covering the development of two large oil concessions, oil shipments and the construction of two pipelines.[362] In addition, China imports an increasing amount of oil and natural gas from the Persian Gulf states.

To sum up, China does not have enough oil and gas reserves to sustain its stunning levels of projected development. Secure oil supplies from the energy-rich Persian Gulf states have become a strategic concern for Beijing. This growing oil dependence has significant implications on a potential Chinese role in the security system in the Persian Gulf.

In the near future, Chinese policy in the region is likely to take two directions. First, China will increase its arms sales to the eight Gulf states. In the 1980s, Beijing supplied both Baghdad and Tehran with all kinds of weapons in their long war against each other and provided Saudi Arabia with CSS-2 intermediate-range missiles. Like Western powers, selling arms to offset oil costs (the re-cycling of petro-dollars) is likely to be an important goal of Chinese policy. Second, China is likely to consolidate its already close cooperation with Iran and Iraq. These two countries have been called "rogue states" by Washington for most of the 1990s and consequently they have been trying to break the isolation. Cooperation with a global power like China would serve this purpose. At the same time, together Iran and Iraq hold about 20 percent of world oil proven reserves. In other words they have the energy resources to meet China's growing consumption. In addition to Russia and North Korea, China is a major supplier of arms to Iran. Moreover, over the years Beijing has helped Tehran to develop its missile programs and some other non-conventional weapons. Washington has always been especially concerned over the Sino-Iranian nuclear collaboration. Under American pressure, China decided to halt its cooperation with Iran in these areas.[363]

---

[361] British Petroleum Company, *BP Statistical Review of World Energy*, London, British Petroleum Company, 1998, p.10.

[362] Energy Economist, "*Pipelines 'R' Us*," No.160, October 1997, p.19.

[363] In October 1997 China told the United States that its nuclear cooperation deal with Iran has been stalled and cruise missile sales will be halted. In addition, an

Meanwhile, China National Petroleum Corporation (CNPC) signed an agreement with the Iraqi government to develop the al-Ahdab field once sanctions are lifted.[364] In other words, China (like Russia and several European companies) is positioning itself to play an active role in the post-sanctions Iraqi oil industry. In short, China is projected to be more assertive in advancing and securing its energy needs in the Persian Gulf. This should further intensify the competition with the United States, Europe, and Russia.

CONCLUSION

At the dawn of a new millennium, there is a growing consensus among the major global powers that the availability of Persian Gulf oil in reliable volume and at reasonable prices is an important key for their prosperity as individual states and for the stability of the international economic system. Given the projected increasing share of Gulf oil in the total world oil production in the foreseeable future, the region's strategic significance will rise even further. Put differently, the political and financial competition by foreign powers is likely to intensify. Each would try to gain more leverage at the expense of the others. For example, a tight oil market could compel an external power to forge special bonds with individual Gulf states to gain privileged or guaranteed access to inexpensive oil.[365]

Threats to the security of the Persian Gulf by a regional actor in alliance with or support from a foreign power should not be ruled out. The region is pregnant with all sources of conflict including ethnicity, sectarianism, shortage of water, and asymmetrical distribution of wealth and power. These cleavages can be used by a foreign power to advance its own individual interests at the expense of other regional and international players. Such a policy would lead to a deepen instability. A more promising approach is coordinated efforts by the global powers to reconcile their energy and security

---

agreement for "peaceful use of nuclear energy" has not been carried out. See *Middle East Economic Digest*, Vol.41, No.44, October 31, 1997, p.14.

[364] United States Department of Energy, Energy Information Administration, Country Report: Iraq, Washington DC: US Government Printing Office, 1998, p.9.

[365] Graham E. Fuller and Ian O. Lesser, "Persian Gulf Myths," *Foreign Affairs*, Vol.76, No.3, May/June 1997, p.49.

policies in the Persian Gulf. This should contribute to a long-term peace and prosperity to all states within and outside the region.

INDEX

D

E

F

G

H

I